PULSE OF A NATION

Health Politics and Trump Phenomenon

DR. DALAL AKOURY, M.D.

Copyright © 224 Dr. Dalal Akoury

PULSE OF A NATION

All rights reserved. No part of this publication may be reproduced, distributed, or transmitted in any form or by any means, including photocopying, recording, or other electronic or mechanical methods, without the prior written permission of the publisher, except in the case of brief quotations embodied in critical reviews and certain other noncommercial uses permitted by copyright law. For permission requests, write to the publisher, addressed "Attention: Permissions Coordinator," at info@beyondpublishing.net

Quantity sales and special discounts are available on quantity purchases by corporations, associations, and others. For details, contact the publisher at the address above.

Orders by U.S. trade bookstores and wholesalers. Email info@ BeyondPublishing.net

The Beyond Publishing Speakers Bureau can bring authors to your live event. For more information or to book an event contact the Beyond Publishing Speakers Bureau speak@BeyondPublishing.net

The Author can be reached directly at BeyondPublishing.net

Manufactured and printed in the United States of America distributed globally by BeyondPublishing.net

New York | Los Angeles | London | Sydney

ISBN Softcover: 978-1-63792-672-7
ISBN Hardcover: 978-1-63792-671-0

DEDICATION

To my beloved husband, Dr. Samy Akoury, whose unwavering support and love have been my anchor through every chapter of life. Your dedication to medicine and our family has inspired me every day.

To my sons, Dr. Tamer Akoury and Dr. Nader Akoury, whose passion for healthcare and commitment to making the world a better place has filled our lives with pride. Dr. Nader Akoury, with his Doctorate in AI, continues to push the boundaries of innovation in medicine and technology. Your journeys have been remarkable, and I am excited to see the impact you will make.

To our great nation, and to the vision of unity, where the Democratic Party and the Republican Party, together with the people, strive for a brighter future. May we continue to work together to build a stronger, more prosperous America.

Table of Contents

Acknowledgments 11
Prologue 13
Introduction 15
1. Introduce the topic and purpose of the book.
2. Highlight the importance of healthcare and doctors' perspectives in the political arena.

Chapter 1: Trump's Healthcare Policies 26
1. Explore President Trump's approach to healthcare reform.
2. Highlight specific policies that have benefitted doctors and healthcare workers.

Chapter 2: Deregulation and Medical Innovation 38
1. Discuss how Trump's deregulation efforts have stimulated medical innovation.
2. Provide examples of deregulatory actions in healthcare.

Chapter 3: Taxation and the Medical Community 50
1. Examine Trump's tax policies and their impact on healthcare professionals.
2. Highlight tax reforms that may have benefited doctors.

Chapter 4: Judicial Appointments 64
1. Analyze Trump's judicial nominations and their implications for healthcare-related cases.
2. Discuss the impact of these appointments on medical ethics and liability.

Chapter 5: International Healthcare Comparisons 73
1. Compare the U.S. healthcare system to international models.

2. Evaluate Trump's approach in the context of global healthcare.

Chapter 6: Personal Experiences and Testimonials (Part 1) 76

1. Share anecdotes and testimonials from doctors who support President Trump.
2. Explore their reasons for choosing him as their preferred candidate.

Chapter 7: Personal Experiences and Testimonials (Part 2) 81

1. Continue with more personal anecdotes and testimonials from healthcare workers.
2. Highlight diverse perspectives within the medical community.

Chapter 8: Telemedicine and Healthcare Access 86

1. Discuss Trump's policies related to telemedicine and healthcare access.
2. Explain how these policies have impacted doctors and patients.

Chapter 9: Drug Pricing and Pharmaceutical Industry 92

1. Examine Trump's efforts to lower drug prices and their reception in the medical community.
2. Discuss the influence of pharmaceutical companies on healthcare policy.

Chapter 10: Mental Health and Veterans' Care 103

1. Explore Trump's initiatives related to mental health and veterans' healthcare.
2. Analyze the impact on healthcare workers treating veterans.

Chapter 11: Public Health and the Pandemic 112

1. Evaluate the Trump administration's response to the COVID-19 pandemic.
2. Discuss how healthcare professionals viewed the handling of public health crises.

Chapter 12: Medical Education and Research Funding 119
1. Examine Trump's policies on medical education and research funding.
2. Explain their effects on the medical profession's future.

Chapter 13: Ethics in Healthcare 123
1. Discuss medical ethics and how they relate to President Trump's policies.
2. Address controversies and debates within the medical community.

Chapter 14: Physician Burnout and Work-Life Balance 133
1. Address physician burnout and work-life balance in the context of Trump's policies.
2. Explain how these policies may have impacted healthcare workers' well-being.

Chapter 15: Rural Healthcare and Access 139
1. Explore challenges in rural healthcare and Trump's initiatives to address them.
2. Share doctors' perspectives on improving rural healthcare.

Chapter 16: Medical Liability and Malpractice Reform 145
1. Analyze the impact of Trump's policies on medical liability and malpractice reform.
2. Discuss how doctors view changes in liability laws.

Chapter 17: Patient Advocacy and Doctor-Patient Relationships 152
1. Highlight doctors' roles as patient advocates.
2. Explain how Trump's policies affected doctor-patient relationships.

Chapter 18: Healthcare Technology and Innovation 161
1. Explore advances in healthcare technology during Trump's presidency.

2. Share doctors' reactions to technological changes.

Chapter 19: The Future of Healthcare 171
1. Speculate on the future of healthcare policy in the U.S.
2. Discuss doctors' hopes and concerns.

Chapter 20: Healthcare Disparities 180
1. Address healthcare disparities under the Trump administration.
2. Explain doctors' perspectives on reducing disparities.

Chapter 21: Medical Research and Breakthroughs 188
1. Discuss Trump's impact on medical research and breakthroughs.
2. Share doctors' reactions to advancements in healthcare science.

Chapter 22: Women's Health and Reproductive Rights 193
1. Explore Trump's policies on women's health and reproductive rights.
2. Discuss how healthcare professionals viewed these policies.

Chapter 23: LGBTQ+ Healthcare 200
1. Analyze Trump's stance on LGBTQ+ healthcare issues.
2. Share doctors' perspectives on LGBTQ+ healthcare access and rights.

Chapter 24: Global Health and International Aid 205
1. Discuss Trump's approach to global health and international aid.
2. Explore how healthcare professionals view global health initiatives.

Chapter 25: Comparing Trump and Biden (Doctors' Perspective) 211
1. Provide a comparative analysis of Trump and Biden's healthcare policies.
2. Emphasize reasons why doctors and healthcare workers may have reservations about voting for Biden.

Conclusion 217
1. Summarize the key points made throughout the book.
2. Encourage readers to engage in informed discussions about healthcare and politics.

About the Author 219

ACKNOWLEDGMENTS

I am deeply grateful to everyone who contributed to the creation of this book, directly or indirectly. Your support and encouragement have been invaluable, and I want to express my heartfelt thanks to each of you.

First and foremost, I want to thank my family – my husband, Dr. Samy Akoury, and my sons, Dr. Tamer Akoury and Dr. Nader Akoury. Your unwavering support and understanding during the long hours of writing and research were the foundation of this book. Your dedication to our family and our country inspires me every day.

I extend my gratitude to the medical community, especially the doctors, nurses, and healthcare professionals who shared their stories and insights. Your experiences shaped the narrative of this book and shed light on the crucial intersection of healthcare and politics.

I would also like to acknowledge the patients and individuals whose stories are woven throughout these pages. Your courage and resilience in the face of healthcare challenges are a testament to the strength of the human spirit.

To my publisher Michael Butler and the dedicated team who helped bring this book to life, thank you for your expertise, guidance, and unwavering commitment to excellence.

Finally, to my readers, thank you for embarking on this journey with me. I hope this book sparks meaningful conversations and fosters a greater understanding of the complex relationship between healthcare and politics.

With deepest appreciation,

Dalal Akoury, MD

PROLOGUE

A Doctor's Journey Through American Healthcare

In the ever-evolving landscape of American healthcare, I embarked on a journey as a doctor—a journey filled with compassion, challenges, and a deep-seated belief in the transformative power of medicine. From the corridors of bustling hospitals to the quiet moments in the doctor-patient relationship, I witnessed the intricate tapestry of life, health, and policy that defines our nation's healthcare system.

This book reflects the experiences, stories, and insights that have shaped my perspective as a healthcare professional. It is an exploration of the interplay between medicine and politics, policy and practice, and the profound impact these dynamics have on the lives of patients and the dedication of doctors.

As I navigated the complexities of healthcare delivery, I encountered the pivotal moments that defined our nation's healthcare journey. From the policies enacted by the Trump administration to the transformative changes brought about by the Biden administration, this book serves as a comprehensive guide to understanding the political forces that shape the healthcare landscape.

Through personal narratives, interviews, and data-driven analysis, we will delve into the heart of healthcare, exploring topics such as access, affordability, technological innovation, and the pursuit of equitable care.

It is my hope that this book will shed light on the critical issues facing our healthcare system, encourage informed discussions, and inspire a shared vision for a healthier, more united America.

Join me on this journey through the pages of "Medicine, Mater, and Trump: Uniting a Nation's Healthcare," as we uncover the stories, challenges, and triumphs that define American healthcare. Together, we will explore the past, navigate the present, and chart a course for the future of healthcare in our great nation.

INTRODUCTION

In a nation where healthcare is both a fundamental human right and a subject of relentless political debate, "Why Doctors and Healthcare Professionals Should Vote for Trump" ventures into uncharted territory. This book is not merely an exploration of policies and positions; it is a rallying cry for a movement poised to reshape the future of healthcare and the role of medical professionals in the political arena.

As our story begins, the American healthcare system stands at a crossroads, where the decisions made within the hallowed halls of government have profound repercussions on the daily lives of citizens and the practice of medicine itself. Within these pages, readers are not passive observers but active participants in a transformational journey that empowers doctors and healthcare professionals to become catalysts for change.

Amidst the cacophony of political discourse, this book emerges as a manifesto—a manifesto not of divisiveness, but of unity and empowerment. It calls upon doctors and healthcare professionals to transcend party lines, ideological differences, and the complexities of a fragmented healthcare landscape. It beckons them to recognize their unique position as stewards of health, advocates for patients, and drivers of medical innovation.

The premise of this book lies in its unwavering belief that the medical community possesses an inherent power—the power to bridge the gap between the intricacies of healthcare policy and the realities of the clinic. It recognizes that healthcare is not solely a political chessboard but a shared space where doctors and healthcare professionals stand as sentinels of health, wellbeing, and the pursuit of a healthier, more equitable America.

This journey is not passive; it is transformative. It challenges preconceived notions, navigates the complexities of healthcare reform, and examines the very essence of what it means to be a healthcare professional in the 21st century. It underscores the urgency of doctors and healthcare professionals actively engaging in the political process, not as partisan combatants but as advocates for a healthcare system that places patients at its core.

In a world where the boundaries between health and politics blur, this book's premise is a clarion call—a call to transform political discourse into informed action, policy into practice, and division into unity. It invites readers to step beyond the sidelines, to join a movement, and to discover the transformative power of their voices in shaping the future of healthcare in America.

During political discourse and the ever-evolving landscape of healthcare, we invite you to embark on a transformative journey through the pages of "Why Doctors and Healthcare Professionals Should Vote for Trump." This book is not just a collection of words; it is a manifesto for a movement—a movement that seeks to empower doctors and healthcare professionals to actively engage in the political process for the betterment of healthcare in America.

The Power of Healthcare Professionals' Voices

n a world where healthcare transcends mere science and becomes a testament to the enduring human spirit, "The Power of Healthcare Professionals' Voices" embarks on a transformative journey. This book, unlike any other, seeks to amplify the often-underestimated voices of doctors and healthcare professionals. Within its pages, a profound narrative unfolds—one that celebrates the remarkable power vested in these individuals, who are not mere practitioners of medicine but guardians of our nation's health.

As we venture into this exploration, the stage is set with a profound understanding: doctors and healthcare professionals are more than healers of physical ailments. They are the custodians of life, the champions of compassion, and the advocates for the most vulnerable among us. They bear a responsibility that extends beyond the confines of a hospital room; it reaches into the heart of communities and the fabric of our society.

This book serves as a beacon—a beacon that illuminates the path towards understanding the significance of healthcare professionals in shaping not only the healthcare landscape but also the very essence of our society. It is a tribute to those who have dedicated their lives to the service of others, who have embraced the oath to "do no harm" as a lifelong commitment, and who have chosen the noble path of alleviating suffering, preserving life, and advocating for the welfare of patients.

"The Power of Healthcare Professionals' Voices" does not simply recount tales of medical practice; it delves into the heart of the medical profession itself. It acknowledges the sacrifices made, the triumphs celebrated, and the challenges faced by healthcare professionals daily. It underscores that the white coat is not just a symbol but a beacon of hope—a symbol of healing, empathy, and resilience.

This premise is unique because it recognizes that healthcare professionals are not merely individuals in white coats; they are the unsung heroes who, through their knowledge, compassion, and dedication, hold the power to shape the healthcare narrative, challenge the status quo, and drive transformation in the delivery of healthcare services.

As we turn the pages of this book, we will encounter stories of resilience, innovation, and advocacy. We will explore the impact of healthcare professionals on the lives of patients, communities, and the broader healthcare ecosystem. We will celebrate their voices—the voices that advocate for patients' rights, advocate for the underserved, and advocate for positive change in healthcare policy.

In a world where healthcare has transcended the boundaries of science and become a reflection of our shared humanity, this book is not just a tribute; it is an invitation—an invitation to recognize and celebrate the immense power that lies within the voices of doctors and healthcare professionals. It is a testament to the enduring spirit of those who dedicate their lives to the pursuit of healing, and it serves as a call to action for society to listen, understand, and amplify the voices that hold the promise of a healthier, more compassionate world.

Within these pages, we will unveil the remarkable power that lies within the voices of doctors and healthcare professionals. We recognize that these individuals are not just healers but guardians of our nation's health, bearing the immense responsibility of preserving life, alleviating suffering, and advocating for the welfare of patients. This book acknowledges and celebrates the significant role healthcare professionals play in shaping the healthcare landscape and our society at large.

The Political Arena and Healthcare

In an era defined by political polarization, where the fault lines of ideology shape the very bedrock of our nation's discourse, "The Political Arena and Healthcare" invites readers to embark on an illuminating journey. This section of the book unfolds against the backdrop of a society grappling with divisions that cut deep, where healthcare and politics, like intertwined destinies, converge at the crossroads of our nation's conscience.

As we delve into the intricate relationship between healthcare and politics, we find ourselves on a quest—to navigate the labyrinthine corridors of healthcare policy with the precision of a surgeon's hand, to chart a course through turbulent waters where political agendas collide with the sacred oath of medicine, and to unveil the profound consequences of decisions made within the hallowed halls of government.

The essence of this section lies not in advocating for a singular viewpoint but in the pursuit of a comprehensive and balanced understanding. It is a journey through the heart of a nation's healthcare policy, revealing that every decision made in the political arena has a ripple effect—a resonance that reverberates through the sterile walls of examination rooms, the bustling corridors of hospitals, and into the very lives of millions.

Here, readers are not passive observers but active participants in the unraveling drama of healthcare and politics. It is an odyssey that dissects the complexities of healthcare reform, the intricacies of insurance systems, and the ethical dilemmas faced by healthcare professionals. It presents an opportunity to explore the nuanced perspectives of doctors, nurses, and healthcare workers who navigate the turbulent waters of policy implementation, patient care, and the ever-evolving landscape of medical practice.

In a society where every vote cast echoes through the halls of power, this section is a beacon—a source of enlightenment, debate, and insight. It invites readers to engage in a dialogue that transcends party lines, to challenge assumptions, and to uncover the multifaceted nature of healthcare politics. Here, healthcare is not a mere political chessboard but a canvas where the colors of compassion, ethics, and innovation merge to create a tapestry of shared values and aspirations.

As we navigate this complex terrain, we embark on a mission—to unravel the intricate dance between healthcare and politics, to illuminate the juncture where the oath to heal converges with the call to govern, and to empower readers with the knowledge to make informed decisions in the ever-evolving landscape of healthcare policy.

In a world where healthcare is both a human right and a political battleground, "The Political Arena and Healthcare" stands as a testament to the enduring power of discourse, knowledge, and empathy—a section that challenges readers to explore the profound intersection of healthcare and politics, forging a path toward understanding and enlightenment in an era defined by division.

In a nation where political divisions run deep, the intersection of healthcare and politics has never been more profound. The purpose of this book is to navigate this intersection, to chart a course through the turbulent waters of healthcare policy, and to shed light on the ways in which the decisions made in the political arena reverberate through examination rooms, hospitals, and the lives of millions. Our objective is not to impose a singular viewpoint but to provide a comprehensive and balanced understanding of why some doctors and healthcare workers may find compelling reasons to support President Donald J. Trump.

The Divided Landscape

In a nation where the tapestry of opinions is as diverse as the colors of a sunset, our medical community stands as a microcosm of this profound diversity. Within the ranks of doctors and healthcare professionals, we find individuals whose political beliefs span a spectrum as broad as the horizon itself. It is a mosaic of thought, where every tile represents a unique perspective, a distinct philosophy, and a deeply held conviction.

"The Divided Landscape" is an invitation to traverse this intricate terrain—a terrain marked not by trenches of ideological warfare but by the rich tapestry of contrasting viewpoints. In recognizing the diversity within the medical community, this section of the book is a testament to the belief that every voice deserves its moment in the spotlight, every perspective deserves a seat at the table, and every opinion is a brushstroke in the portrait of our healthcare discourse.

Here, readers will not find an attempt to impose a singular viewpoint or to sway opinion with the force of persuasion. Instead, they are welcomed into an environment where the multifaceted nature of healthcare politics is explored with a spirit of curiosity and respect. This is not a battlefield; it is a forum—a place where the richness of dialogue, the exchange of ideas, and the illumination of different angles coalesce into an intellectual mosaic.

Within "The Divided Landscape," the canvas is painted with the colors of civil discourse, where the clash of ideas is not a thunderous storm but a symphony of voices. It is a celebration of the intellectual diversity within the medical profession—a celebration that recognizes the strength of a community that thrives on the exchange of ideas and the pursuit of knowledge.

As readers navigate this section, they are encouraged to embrace the plurality of thought that defines our society. It is an opportunity to explore the multifaceted nature of healthcare politics, to engage with perspectives that may differ from their own, and to emerge with a deeper understanding of the complex and often paradoxical nature of our healthcare system.

In an era where the cacophony of political discord can be deafening, "The Divided Landscape" stands as an oasis—a place of intellectual refuge, where readers can pause, reflect, and engage in constructive dialogue. It is a reminder that diversity of thought is not a source of division but a wellspring of innovation, where every perspective contributes to the ongoing evolution of our healthcare discourse.

In traversing this divided landscape, readers will embark on a journey of discovery—an exploration that transcends the boundaries of ideology, fosters an environment of respect, and reinforces the belief that, in the mosaic of diverse perspectives, lies the true beauty of our intellectual landscape.

The Journey Ahead

As you traverse the chapters ahead, you will embark on a profound journey of discovery. We will delve into the policies, actions, and initiatives undertaken during the Trump administration, dissecting their impact on medical practice, patient care, and the broader healthcare ecosystem. Each chapter serves as a beacon, illuminating specific reasons that have led some within the medical community to align their votes with President Trump. This journey is not a passive one; it is an invitation to actively engage with the intersection of healthcare and politics.

Call to Engagement

In these pivotal moments, as we collectively strive to navigate the complex and intricate relationship between healthcare and politics, we extend a call to engagement. We urge you, the reader, to approach this book with an open heart and a commitment to understanding. A movement is not defined by its leaders alone; it is propelled by the collective action of its members. Let this book serve as a catalyst—a spark that ignites the passion of doctors and healthcare professionals to participate in the democratic process actively.

Conclusion of the Introduction Chapter

"In the Heart of the Healthcare Revolution: A Movement for Change"

As the final pages of "Why Doctors and Healthcare Professionals Should Vote for Trump" turn, a powerful transformation takes hold. This book transcends the boundaries of mere literature; it evolves into a movement—an extraordinary, purpose-driven force that recognizes healthcare professionals as the vanguards of our society. It is an acknowledgment that the future of healthcare and the well-being of every citizen lie in the hands of those who have dedicated their lives to the noble art of healing.

"In the Heart of the Healthcare Revolution" is more than just a conclusion; it is the inception of a journey that beckons readers to become architects of change. This is a movement that recognizes the critical role healthcare professionals play in our society—an acknowledgment that their knowledge, compassion, and dedication are the pillars upon which a healthier America can be built.

In these concluding pages, we stand on the precipice of transformation, with open hearts and inquisitive minds. It is a transformative journey that empowers readers to become active participants in the democratic process, advocates for policy reform, and champions of a healthcare system that serves all members of society.

This movement is driven by the belief that doctors and healthcare professionals are not just healers of bodies; they are healers of systems, architects of policy, and beacons of hope. It is a recognition that informed political engagement is not a choice but a responsibility—a responsibility to ensure that the healthcare landscape is one that prioritizes the welfare of patients, the dignity of caregivers, and the pursuit of excellence in medical practice.

As we embark on this transformative journey together, we recognize that the future of healthcare in the United States is not predetermined; it is a canvas awaiting the brushstrokes of change. It is a call to action that resonates with the belief that, in unity and with determination, doctors, nurses, and healthcare professionals can shape a healthcare system that is equitable, accessible, and compassionate.

"In the Heart of the Healthcare Revolution" invites readers to stand at the forefront of a movement—a movement that seeks to bridge the gap between healthcare and politics, to transform divisions into dialogues, and to advocate for a healthcare system that places the wellbeing of every citizen at its heart.

In these concluding moments, we embark on a transformative journey—a journey that extends beyond the confines of this book, beyond the boundaries of politics, and into the heart of a healthcare revolution. It is a movement that invites readers to carry the torch of change, to be the advocates of progress, and to shape a future where healthcare is not just a privilege but a right for all.

Inciting incident

"In the midst of a tumultuous political climate, I, Dr. Dalal Akoury, MD a concerned citizen and healthcare advocate, found myself pondering the intersection of healthcare and politics. It was a pivotal moment when I realized that the decisions made in the political arena had a profound impact on the lives of doctors, patients, and the entire healthcare system. This realization ignited my passion to explore the stories, challenges, and triumphs of healthcare professionals who navigate this complex landscape daily. It became clear that their experiences needed to be shared, and their voices needed to be heard."

This inciting incident not only introduces you as the author and your motivation for writing the book but also sets the stage for the exploration of healthcare and politics from the perspective of doctors and healthcare professionals.

CHAPTER 1

TRUMP'S HEALTHCARE POLICIES

"Celebrating Trump's Healing Hands:
Where Policy Meets Compassion, Lives Are Shaped,
and Healthcare is Defined."

Setting the Stage

In the intricate web of American healthcare, where policies have the power to shape lives, influence practices, and chart the course of medicine, we find ourselves at a defining moment in history. Chapter 1, titled "Trump's Healthcare Policies," serves as a portal into the realm of healthcare reform during the Trump administration—a journey that explores the strategic approach and concrete policies that have left an indelible mark on doctors, nurses, and healthcare workers across the nation.

As we begin this chapter, the canvas is blank but not empty. It carries the weight of a nation's expectations, the echoes of past healthcare endeavors, and the aspirations of those who dedicate their lives to the noble art of healing. It is a canvas that invites us to delve into the heart of President Donald J. Trump's vision for healthcare, to uncover the brushstrokes of reform, and to illuminate the specific policies that have cast a spotlight on doctors and healthcare professionals.

The Trumpian Approach to Healthcare Reform

This section of the book is an intellectual journey that seeks to understand President Trump's unique philosophy and vision for healthcare reform. It transcends partisan politics and delves into the foundational principles that guided his administration's healthcare policies. This vision is characterized by a commitment to prioritizing patient access, promoting innovation, and supporting healthcare practitioners. It has sparked debates and discussions that go beyond party lines, inviting readers to explore the fundamental values that underlie the future of American healthcare. "Reimagining Healthcare" is an invitation to engage with these ideas, challenge assumptions, and participate in shaping a healthcare system that places patients, caregivers, and innovation at its core. In the intricate labyrinth of American healthcare, where the paths of policy intersect with the lives of millions, we embark on an intellectual odyssey—an exploration that transcends the partisan divide. This section, titled "Reimagining Healthcare," invites readers to delve into the very essence of President Donald J. Trump's vision for reforming healthcare—a vision that defies categorization along political lines.

As we navigate this journey, we are not passive spectators but active seekers of understanding. Our quest is to unravel the underlying philosophy that served as the North Star for President Trump's approach to healthcare reform. It is a philosophy that resonates with the belief in a healthcare system that places patients and practitioners at the forefront—a system that prioritizes accessibility, innovation, and the welfare of those who dedicate their lives to the noble art of healing.

This is not merely an examination of policies but an expedition into the soul of healthcare—a journey that unearths the foundational principles upon which the administration's policies were built. We explore a vision that challenges conventions, ignites debates, and stirs the cauldron of discourse on the future of American healthcare.

In the pages that follow, we encounter a vision that is as diverse as the nation itself—a vision that has evoked passionate responses and ignited robust discussions. It is a vision that raises questions, sparks debates, and fuels the discourse on the path forward for healthcare. It is a vision that invites readers to transcend the boundaries of party politics and to consider the fundamental values that underpin the reform of healthcare in the United States.

As we delve into this exploration, we will encounter the spectrum of ideas that have shaped the Trumpian approach to healthcare reform. Each idea is a brushstroke on the canvas, a stroke that reflects the multifaceted nature of healthcare in America. We will navigate the complexities, ponder the implications, and engage with the very essence of what it means to reimagine healthcare in the 21st century.

In the end, "Reimagining Healthcare" is not just a section; it is an invitation—an invitation to engage with the intellectual tapestry of healthcare reform, to challenge preconceptions, and to explore a vision that transcends party lines and rekindles the discourse on the future of American healthcare. It is a journey that beckons readers to join in the pursuit of a healthcare system that places the wellbeing of patients, the dignity of caregivers, and the promise of innovation at its core.

It seeks to uncover the underlying philosophy that guided his approach of President Trump's approach to healthcare reform emphasizing principles that transcend political affiliations. The vision prioritizes patient-centered care, accessibility, innovation, and the welfare of healthcare professionals. It sparks debates, raises questions, and rekindles discourse on the future of American healthcare. Readers are invited to transcend partisan lines, explore the foundational values of healthcare reform, and engage with diverse ideas that have shaped this approach. Ultimately, it's an exploration of the multifaceted nature of healthcare in the United States and an invitation to reimagine the healthcare landscape for the 21st century.

Policies that Empowered Healthcare Professionals

Within this section, we dive into the heart of Trump's healthcare policies, seeking to uncover the policies that directly impacted doctors, nurses, and healthcare workers. Each policy becomes a brushstroke on the canvas, a stroke that highlights the profound influence of these policies on the medical community. We explore how these policies have not only shaped the practice of medicine but have also, in tangible ways, benefited the healthcare professionals who stand on the front lines of patient care.

In this exploration, we are not passive observers but active participants in the narrative of healthcare reform. We stand shoulder to shoulder with healthcare professionals who have witnessed the impact of these policies firsthand, who have grappled with the complexities of reform, and who have experienced the ripple effect in their daily work.

As we delve deeper into this chapter, it becomes evident that Trump's healthcare policies are not just a series of decisions; they are the embodiment of a vision—a vision for a healthcare system that prioritizes accessibility, innovation, and the welfare of patients and caregivers alike.

In the pages that follow, we will navigate the intricacies of specific policies, examine their implications, and hear the voices of those who have been touched by these reforms. Together, we will uncover the canvas, illuminate the brushstrokes, and paint a comprehensive picture of President Trump's approach to healthcare reform and its direct impact on doctors and healthcare workers across the nation.

Here is an overview of some of the key healthcare policies and initiatives during the Trump administration:

1. **Repeal and Replace of the Affordable Care Act (ACA):**

    One of the major healthcare policy goals of President Trump was to repeal and replace the Affordable Care Act, commonly known as Obamacare. While efforts to fully repeal the ACA were unsuccessful, some provisions were modified or eliminated through legislative actions.

2. **Expansion of Short-Term Health Plans:**

    The Trump administration expanded the availability of short-term health insurance plans. These plans typically offer lower premiums but may provide less comprehensive coverage compared to ACA-compliant plans. Supporters argued that this provided more choice for consumers, while critics raised concerns about potential coverage gaps.

3. **Expansion of Health Savings Accounts (HSAs):**

    The administration took steps to expand Health Savings Accounts, allowing individuals to save more pre-tax dollars for healthcare expenses. This was seen to increase consumer control over healthcare spending.

4. **Medicaid Work Requirements:**

    The Trump administration encouraged states to implement work requirements for Medicaid beneficiaries. Several states sought approval to require certain Medicaid recipients to work, volunteer, or participate in job training as a condition for eligibility. Legal challenges and varying opinions on the effectiveness of such requirements arose.

5. **Price Transparency Executive Order:**
   President Trump signed an executive order aimed at increasing price transparency in the healthcare system. The order required hospitals and insurers to disclose their negotiated prices for services, allowing patients to make more informed decisions about their care.

6. **Drug Pricing Reforms:**
   The Trump administration pursued several initiatives to lower prescription drug prices, including efforts to increase competition among drug manufacturers, importation of cheaper drugs from other countries, and ending drug rebates to pharmacy benefit managers (PBMs).

7. **Efforts to Combat the Opioid Epidemic:**
   The Trump administration declared the opioid crisis a public health emergency and took various actions to address it, including increased funding for addiction treatment, expanding access to overdose-reversal medication, and implementing stricter prescribing guidelines.

8. **COVID-19 Response:**
   While the COVID-19 pandemic began during President Trump's term, his administration played a significant role in the response. Initiatives included Operation Warp Speed to accelerate vaccine development, distribution of relief funds to healthcare providers, and efforts to expand telehealth access during the pandemic.

9. **Right to Try Act:**
   The Right to Try Act was signed into law by President Trump in 2018. This legislation allows terminally ill patients who have exhausted all approved treatment options to access experimental

treatments that have not yet received full approval from the Food and Drug Administration (FDA). The law aimed to provide patients with greater access to potentially life-saving treatments and reduce bureaucratic hurdles in obtaining experimental drugs.

The Right to Try Act was seen as a significant policy change, granting patients more autonomy and the opportunity to pursue experimental treatments when facing life-threatening illnesses. It was considered a move toward expanding patient choice and access to innovative therapies. However, it also raised concerns about patient safety and the effectiveness of experimental treatments that had not undergone rigorous FDA testing.

"Healing Hands Empowered: Unveiling the Real-World Impact on Doctors and Healthcare Workers" The Impact of Trumpian policies on Doctors and Providers

As we delve into the transformative landscape of President Trump's healthcare policies, it becomes evident that the changes implemented had a profound impact on the livelihood and financial freedom of doctors and healthcare providers. This section serves as a spotlight on the consequences, both intended and unintended, of the healthcare reform initiatives championed during this administration.

Exploring the Financial Implications: Within this section, we navigate the financial ramifications of the policies set in motion. Doctors and healthcare providers found themselves at the intersection of reimbursement adjustments, regulatory changes, and shifts in the healthcare marketplace. As the healthcare system evolved, practitioners experienced shifts in revenue models, coding and billing practices, and the overall financial landscape of their practices.

The Balancing Act: One of the central themes that emerges is the delicate balancing act that doctors and providers faced. On one hand, certain policies aimed to streamline administrative burdens and improve the efficiency of healthcare delivery, potentially freeing up resources and reducing costs. On the other hand, changes in reimbursement rates, compliance requirements, and insurance dynamics introduced new challenges. Healthcare professionals had to adapt to a rapidly evolving environment while managing the economic sustainability of their practices.

The Quest for Financial Freedom: Amidst the transformation, doctors and providers embarked on a quest for financial freedom. This section delves into their entrepreneurial spirit, exploring how healthcare professionals sought innovative strategies to maintain financial stability, explore new revenue streams, and adapt to the evolving landscape. It highlights the stories of those who successfully navigated the changes and the lessons learned from their experiences.

Unintended Consequences and Challenges: It's important to acknowledge the unintended consequences and challenges faced by healthcare professionals during this period of transformation. Some practitioners encountered hurdles related to reimbursement delays, shifts in patient demographics, or the complexities of transitioning to value-based care models. These challenges underscored the resilience and adaptability required in the face of healthcare reform.

Looking Ahead: The section concludes by peering into the future. As the healthcare system continues to evolve, doctors and providers must remain vigilant and proactive in adapting to new policies, technology advancements, and patient expectations. The financial landscape of healthcare remains a dynamic terrain, and healthcare professionals are poised to play a pivotal role in shaping its direction.

In examining the effect of transformation on doctors and providers' livelihood and financial freedom, this section offers a comprehensive view of the real-world impact of healthcare policies. It highlights the resilience of healthcare professionals and their ability to adapt to change, while also acknowledging the challenges they face in maintaining their financial well-being amidst a shifting healthcare landscape.

In the vast landscape of healthcare policy, it's easy to become entangled in the web of legislative jargon and bureaucratic maneuvers. However, this section, titled "Healing Hands Empowered," is a dedicated space where the spotlight shifts to the true heroes of healthcare—the doctors and healthcare workers whose unwavering dedication and compassionate care form the foundation of the entire system.

Here, the story isn't confined to the pages of policy documents; it springs to life, vivid and tangible. It's a narrative of how healthcare policies, born in the corridors of power, took root in the everyday lives of those who stand at the frontline of patient well-being. It's a tale of transformation, empowerment, support, and the profound recognition of the invaluable contributions made by doctors and healthcare workers.

We embark on a journey to uncover the real-world impact of these policies on the medical community—a community that heals, nurtures, and perseveres in the face of adversity. Each policy becomes a beacon, illuminating the path toward a better healthcare ecosystem—one that not only values the dedication and sacrifices of healthcare professionals but also actively supports their mission to heal and comfort.

Championing the Healing Hands: This section is a tribute to the healing hands that tirelessly work to mend broken bodies and spirits. It explores how healthcare policies translated into tangible benefits for doctors and healthcare workers, enhancing their ability to deliver quality care. It delves into the stories of practitioners who found themselves empowered and supported by policies that recognized their pivotal role in healthcare.

A Tale of Empowerment: The narrative unfolds as we discover how policies have empowered doctors and healthcare workers to practice medicine with greater autonomy, reduced administrative burdens, and improved access to necessary resources. It emphasizes the transformation of healthcare professionals from mere service providers to advocates for their patients and champions of a more efficient healthcare system.

Recognition and Support: In the pages that follow, we celebrate the policies that have recognized the tireless efforts of healthcare workers and extended support where it was needed most. It highlights instances where policies facilitated professional growth, enhanced the work environment, and ensured that the wellbeing of those on the frontlines was a priority.

Beyond the Policy Papers: This section goes beyond the dry ink of policy papers and delves into the living, breathing experiences of doctors and healthcare workers. It brings to life the moments of triumph, the challenges faced, and the enduring commitment to the oath of healing. It serves as a testament to the resilience and dedication of those who dedicate their lives to the service of others.

"Healing Hands Empowered" is more than a section; it is a tribute—a tribute to the healthcare professionals who have tirelessly served, innovated, and persevered. It is an exploration of how policies transformed the landscape of their work, how support elevated their mission, and how recognition fortified their commitment. In these pages, we witness the profound impact of healthcare policies on the lives of those who embody the spirit of healing.

"The Trumpian Healthcare Odyssey: A Prelude to the Healthcare-Political Nexus"

As we reach the closing moments of Chapter 1, we find ourselves at a juncture—a juncture where we've journeyed through the intricate labyrinth of Trump's healthcare policies. We've traversed his vision, dissected the policies, and witnessed their tangible impacts on the healthcare landscape. This chapter is more than an introduction; it's the cornerstone, the threshold, and the compass that guides our path into the heart of healthcare's entanglement with the political arena.

This is an odyssey—an odyssey that has just begun. It's a journey that weaves the threads of policy, vision, and consequence into a narrative tapestry that will unravel with each turn of the page. We've set the stage, illuminated the backdrop, and introduced the characters—doctors, healthcare workers, policymakers, and patients—all poised at the center of a healthcare-political nexus that is as multifaceted as it is vital.

In the pages to come, we will venture deeper into this nexus, exploring the complexities, contradictions, and collaborations that define the relationship between healthcare and the political arena. We'll witness the clashes of ideology, the convergence of interests, and the far-reaching implications of decisions made in the hallowed halls of power.

But for now, as we bid farewell to Chapter 1, we carry with us the foundational knowledge that President Trump's healthcare policies were more than ink on paper; they were strokes on a canvas, shaping the landscape of healthcare for doctors, healthcare workers, and patients alike. We embark on a journey of understanding, curiosity, and introspection—a journey that seeks to unveil the intricacies of healthcare in the United States and its undeniable entanglement with the political currents of our time.

In the chapters ahead, we will delve deeper, question more, and explore the diverse perspectives that make up the tapestry of healthcare in America. We'll navigate the twists and turns of policy, ideology, and pragmatism, all while keeping our compass firmly aligned with the enduring goal of healthcare—improving lives, healing wounds, and championing the welfare of every citizen.

As we turn the page and step into the next chapter, we carry the knowledge that our odyssey is only beginning—an odyssey that seeks to unravel the complexities, the triumphs, and the challenges that define the ever-evolving relationship between healthcare and the political arena in the United States.

CHAPTER 2

DEREGULATION AND MEDICAL INNOVATION

"Under President Trump, we broke free from regulatory constraints, ignited innovation, and charted the future of healthcare. Join us on this exhilarating journey!" 🚀

"Unshackling Innovation: Where Deregulation Fuels the Fires of Medical Progress"

Here, we uncover the tangible actions taken by the Trump administration to unshackle the shackles that had bound medical innovation. We spotlight examples of deregulation in healthcare, each serving as a pivotal moment where the regulatory landscape was reshaped to empower innovators, reduce bureaucratic hurdles, and fuel progress.

As we traverse this chapter, we encounter stories of visionaries who saw opportunities in the wake of deregulation—physicians, researchers, entrepreneurs, and institutions that seized the moment to push boundaries, embark on transformative research, and usher in a new era of medical breakthroughs.

In the pages to come, we will witness the real-world impact of deregulation—a ripple effect that stretches from laboratories to hospital rooms, from startups to established institutions. We'll explore the stories of those whose ingenuity was set free by the winds of deregulation, and the profound implications their innovations had on the lives of patients and the future of healthcare.

The canvas before us is no longer blank; it's a canvas filled with the vibrant colors of innovation, a canvas where the brushstrokes of deregulation and medical progress intertwine. In this chapter, we stand on the threshold of discovery, poised to uncover the transformative power of unleashing innovation through deregulation—a power that redefines healthcare, shapes the future, and offers a glimpse into the boundless potential of the human spirit.

As we embark on this journey through the corridors of medical innovation, we invite you to walk alongside us, to explore the possibilities that emerge when the constraints of regulation are eased, and the creative energies of the medical community are unleashed. It's a journey that celebrates the indomitable spirit of innovation and the enduring belief that, in the quest for better healthcare, the sky is not the limit; it's the starting point.

As we venture further into the intricate tapestry of Trump's healthcare legacy, we find ourselves at a crossroads—a chapter that serves as a beacon illuminating the intersection of deregulation and medical innovation. It's a chapter that invites us to explore the vibrant dance between policy reforms and the brilliant spark of human ingenuity within the realm of healthcare.

In this unfolding narrative, we traverse into a realm where deregulation emerges as a potent catalyst—a catalyst that breathes life into innovation, fuels groundbreaking strides, and redefines the contours of the healthcare landscape. It's a story that reverberates with the conviction that when excessive regulatory constraints fall away, the seeds of medical innovation find fertile ground to take root and flourish.

Here, the pages are imbued with the energy of transformation, where the lifting of bureaucratic weights unleashes the boundless potential of healthcare visionaries. It's a journey that unveils the synergy between visionary policymaking and the relentless pursuit of progress—a journey that compels us to rethink the boundaries of possibility in the world of medicine.

As we embark on this chapter, we step into a world where regulations recede, and the human spirit soars. It's a world where healthcare is not just an industry but a crucible of innovation, where the dreams of scientists, doctors, and caregivers find wings to soar. The narrative that follows is a testament to the enduring belief that, in the absence of constraints, innovation knows no bounds—a belief that promises to inspire and illuminate the path ahead.

Unleashing the Medical Imagination: Trump's Deregulation and the Dawn of Healthcare Innovation

In this section, we embark on an expedition into the dynamic landscape of healthcare deregulation. We journey through the tangible actions taken during the Trump administration, each a chisel striking at the regulatory barriers that had long stifled innovation. These actions become milestones, illuminating the path to the liberation of medical progress. We venture into a realm where policies are designed to empower not just healthcare professionals but also researchers, entrepreneurs, and visionaries who dare to dream of a brighter healthcare future.

Reduced Regulatory Burden for Electronic Health Records (EHR)

Imagine a world where healthcare providers are free from the burdensome maze of EHR regulations. The Trump administration recognized that the excessive reporting requirements and bureaucratic hurdles associated with Electronic Health Records stifled innovation. By easing the regulatory shackles, they enabled healthcare professionals to focus on what they do best caring for patients. This liberation not only reduced administrative burdens but also paved the way for the evolution of EHR systems, with a greater emphasis on usability, interoperability, and patient engagement.

Expansion of Telehealth Services

In the wake of a global pandemic, the world yearned for accessible and safe healthcare. The Trump administration responded by relaxing regulations around telehealth services. Suddenly, the boundaries of healthcare extended beyond clinic walls and into the digital realm. Doctors could now reach patients in remote areas, and patients could access care from the comfort of their homes. The innovation of telehealth soared as regulatory constraints were set aside, offering a glimpse of a future where healthcare knows no geographical bounds.

Streamlined and Speeding Up FDA Approvals

In the world of medical research and drug development, time is often a critical factor. The Trump administration recognized this and took steps to streamline the FDA approval process for certain medical devices and drugs. By reducing the bureaucratic red tape, they facilitated the rapid deployment of innovative treatments to those in need. The result was a surge in groundbreaking advancements—a testament to what can be achieved when innovation is not impeded by regulatory hurdles.

Price Transparency That Empowers Patients

Transparency is a cornerstone of a fair and efficient healthcare system. The introduction of price transparency rules forced the healthcare industry to confront its opacity. By requiring hospitals to disclose negotiated prices and common procedure costs, patients gained the power of informed decision-making. This deregulatory action marked a turning point—a step towards a healthcare system where patients have the knowledge and agency to choose the best care for their needs.

Expansion of Scope of Practice for Nurse Practitioners and Physician Assistants

Access to primary care is a vital component of a functioning healthcare system. The Trump administration recognized that by expanding the scope of practice for nurse practitioners and physician assistants, underserved communities could gain better access to care. This deregulatory move enabled these skilled professionals to deliver a wider range of services, increasing healthcare access and improving patient outcomes in areas previously underserved.

These examples are but a glimpse into the tapestry of innovation unleashed by deregulation during the Trump administration. Each action represents a brushstroke on the canvas of progress—a canvas where the imagination of healthcare professionals and researchers knows no bounds. As we journey through this chapter, we will encounter stories of audacity, discovery, and the boundless potential of human ingenuity—a testament to the dawn of healthcare innovation sparked by the power of deregulation.

The Alchemy of Progress: The essence of this chapter is the alchemy of progress—an exploration of how deregulation has transformed healthcare from a field bound by constraints to one that thrives on possibilities. It's a narrative that captures the essence of innovation as a force that defies limitations, unlocks solutions, and expands the horizons of what is possible in the realm of healthcare.

Turning the Page: This chapter is not just an examination of policies but a turning of the page—a turning toward a future where healthcare innovation knows no bounds. It is an invitation to witness the tangible outcomes of deregulation, to celebrate the trailblazers of medical progress, and to explore the infinite potential that lies ahead.

"The Renaissance of Innovation: Deregulation as the Spark of Medical Progress"

In the chapters that follow, we will immerse ourselves in the stories of inventors, visionaries, and pioneers who have harnessed the power of deregulation to shape the landscape of healthcare innovation. It's a testament to the enduring spirit of exploration, a reminder that, in the absence of regulatory shackles, the human imagination can soar to unprecedented heights.

In this section, we plunge into the heart of deregulation's transformative power as a catalyst for medical innovation. We embark on a journey that dissects the dismantling of bureaucratic hurdles, unveiling how this liberation fuels the entrepreneurial spirit within the healthcare industry. It's a narrative of liberation—a liberation that emboldens the brightest minds in medicine to embark on daring expeditions into uncharted territories, ultimately rewriting the script of patient care.

The Journey Begins: Bureaucratic Barriers Overcome

Our journey commences with an exploration of the stifling bureaucratic barriers that once stood as formidable obstacles to healthcare innovation. We unravel how these regulatory entanglements acted as restraints on the creativity and vision of healthcare professionals. Then, we delve into the pivotal policy shifts that dismantled these barriers, unleashing a torrent of creative energy within the industry.

A New Breed of Entrepreneurs

As we venture further, we encounter a new breed of healthcare entrepreneurs—individuals who, unburdened by excessive regulations, dared to dream and dared to innovate. These visionaries disrupt the status quo, introducing novel solutions and pioneering groundbreaking technologies. Their stories resonate with the belief that deregulation is not merely the removal of constraints; it's the liberation of human potential.

Exploring Uncharted Territories

Our narrative takes us into the uncharted territories of healthcare innovation. We witness the audacious endeavors of doctors, researchers, and entrepreneurs who boldly ventured into unexplored realms of medicine. These pioneers challenge conventions, question boundaries, and reimagine patient care. It's a journey into the unknown, where each step forward carries the promise of transformative change.

Revolutionizing Patient Care

At the heart of our exploration lies the transformation of patient care. We observe how deregulation catalyzes advancements that directly impact the lives of patients. From personalized treatments to more accessible care options, the patient experience is redefined. It's a testament to the boundless potential of healthcare innovation when regulatory shackles are removed.

"Crafting the Future: Unveiling the Blueprint of Healthcare Deregulation"

In this section, we embark on a journey to unveil the tangible examples of deregulatory actions in healthcare. These actions represent the intricate threads of policy reform that wove the fabric of innovation and progress during the Trump administration. From the streamlining of FDA approvals to the alleviation of administrative burdens on medical practitioners, we shine a spotlight on each policy and initiative that boldly reshaped the regulatory landscape. As we explore these actions, we witness how each one serves as a brushstroke on the canvas of innovation—a collective effort that has contributed to a richer, more vibrant tapestry of healthcare progress.

Streamlined FDA Approvals

Our journey commences with a deep dive into the realm of FDA approvals. We examine how the traditional regulatory pathway once posed formidable challenges to the timely delivery of life-saving treatments. Then, we unveil the policies that set-in motion the streamlining of this process, allowing innovative medical devices and drugs to reach patients more swiftly. It's a narrative of how deregulation is fostering an environment where groundbreaking advancements are no longer bogged down by bureaucratic red tape.

Easing Administrative Burdens

Here, we shine a light on the administrative burdens that healthcare professionals once carried on their shoulders. We navigate through the labyrinth of regulations that demanded extensive documentation and compliance, often at the expense of patient care. Then, we reveal how deregulatory actions lightened this burden, allowing doctors and practitioners to redirect their focus to what matters most: their patients. It's a story of how the removal of these constraints has breathed new life into healthcare, where providers can deliver care with greater efficiency and compassion.

Promoting Innovation Hubs

In the final chapter of this section, we explore the concept of innovation hubs. These hubs became the epicenters of creative thinking, collaboration, and cutting-edge research. We uncover the policies that fostered the growth of these hubs, attracting the brightest minds in medicine and technology. It's a narrative of how deregulation has nurtured environments where innovation thrives, where interdisciplinary teams work together to tackle healthcare's most pressing challenges, and where the future of healthcare is being crafted.

In "Crafting the Future," we unearth the blueprint of healthcare deregulation—a blueprint that has catalyzed innovation, eased burdens, and ignited the spirit of collaboration. It is a testament to the belief that through thoughtful policy reform, we can pave the way for a healthcare landscape where progress is not hindered by bureaucracy, but where the pursuit of better, more accessible, and more efficient healthcare is unshackled and allowed to flourish.

Liberating Medical Entrepreneurs

Here, we shine a spotlight on the policies that liberated medical entrepreneurs from the constraints of bureaucracy. We witness the birth of startups and innovations that once faced insurmountable regulatory barriers. It's a narrative of how deregulation became the wind beneath the wings of those daring to reshape the healthcare industry, introducing new solutions, and challenging conventional wisdom.

The final brushstroke on our canvas of progress celebrates the spirit of entrepreneurship within healthcare. We venture into the realm of startups and innovative initiatives that have flourished under deregulation. We witness the birth of solutions that tackle healthcare challenges head-on, from improving patient outcomes to enhancing access to care. It's a story of bold visionaries who saw opportunities in a deregulated landscape and transformed healthcare one innovation at a time.

In "Unveiling the Canvas of Progress," we dissect the tangible actions that reshaped healthcare through deregulation. Each example paints a vivid picture of innovation, efficiency, and progress—a picture that reveals the transformative potential of regulatory reform. This section stands as a testament to the belief that when the blueprint of healthcare embraces change, the canvas becomes a masterpiece of advancement and a source of inspiration for the future.

"A Future Defined by Innovation Embracing the Boundless Horizon Shaped by Deregulation and Medical Innovation"

In the final section of this chapter, we transcend the world of policy papers and enter a realm where the future is no longer confined by boundaries but defined by innovation. We embark on a journey that illuminates the enduring impact of deregulation on the trajectory of medical research, patient care, and the ever-expanding horizons of healthcare. It's a glimpse into a world where barriers have crumbled, and the limitless potential of human ingenuity is unleashed.

The Legacy of Deregulation

Our journey begins by tracing the legacy of deregulation—the seeds sown by visionary policy decisions that have blossomed into a landscape defined by innovation. We explore the ripple effects of these decisions, from the laboratories where researchers dream of new cures to the bedside where patients experience the benefits of groundbreaking treatments. It's a testament to how a forward-thinking approach to regulation can shape the destiny of healthcare.

Stories of Breakthroughs

Here, we encounter the stories of breakthroughs—of medical advancements that once seemed unimaginable. We delve into the laboratories and research institutions where scientists have pushed the boundaries of knowledge, and regulatory relief has given them the freedom to dream bigger. It's a narrative of resilience, tenacity, and the unyielding human spirit that refuses to accept the status quo, ushering in an era of unprecedented discoveries.

The Unyielding Human Spirit

In our final brushstroke, we celebrate the unyielding human spirit—the driving force behind the fusion of deregulation and innovation.

We venture into the hearts and minds of healthcare professionals, researchers, and entrepreneurs who dare to defy convention. Their stories embody the boundless possibilities that emerge when regulation yields to innovation, and they serve as a testament to the indomitable spirit that propels healthcare into a future where the sky is not the limit, but just the beginning.

In "Embracing the Boundless Horizon," we celebrate the marriage of deregulation and medical innovation, a union that has given birth to a future where healthcare knows no bounds. This section is a tribute to the power of visionary policy decisions in shaping the destiny of healthcare—a destiny defined not by constraints but by the limitless potential of human ingenuity.

In the final chapters of this section, we peer into the future—a future where deregulation continues to serve as the spark for medical breakthroughs. We explore the endless possibilities that lie ahead, fueled by the unwavering spirit of innovation. It's a narrative of hope, resilience, and the belief that in the absence of bureaucratic constraints, healthcare knows no bounds.

"The Catalyst of Deregulation" is a chapter that celebrates the profound impact of liberation—a liberation that empowers healthcare professionals to envision, create, and push the boundaries of what's possible. It's a journey into a realm where the human spirit soars, innovation flourishes, and the art of healing evolves.

CHAPTER 3

TAXATION AND THE MEDICAL COMMUNITY

"Trump's judicial picks shaped a new era in healthcare, altering ethics, liability, and the patient-care landscape. In Chapter 3, we reveal their impact and the call for change they ignite."

"Balancing the Ledger: Trump's Tax Policies and Their Ripple Effect on Healthcare Professionals"

Chapter 3 invites you to embark on a captivating journey into the intricate relationship between taxation and the medical community during the Trump administration. We peel back the layers of President Trump's tax policies, revealing their profound impact on the lives of healthcare professionals, doctors, and the broader healthcare landscape. This chapter unveils not only the tax reforms that restored financial equilibrium for physicians but also the transformative ripple effect they triggered within the medical community.

Tax Relief for the Healing Hands

Our journey commences with a close examination of the tax relief measures carefully crafted to benefit the healing hands of the medical community. We navigate through the intricate tax policies that lightened the financial burden on doctors and healthcare workers. It's a narrative of economic respite, enabling healthcare professionals to allocate resources more efficiently to their practices, career growth, and patient care.

Fostering the Seeds of Innovation

In the heart of this chapter lies a spotlight on tax incentives that nurtured innovation within the healthcare realm. We explore the fiscal mechanisms designed to fuel creativity and incentivize research. From research and development tax credits to innovative startup incentives, we delve into the fiscal landscape that empowered medical professionals to push boundaries and pioneer transformative advancements. It's a story of how tax policy ignited the flames of medical progress.

Empowering Financial Futures

Our final journey within this chapter navigates the practical strategies employed by doctors and healthcare professionals to navigate the intricate tax landscape. We unlock the financial wisdom and insights that empowered medical practitioners to secure their financial futures while providing unwavering patient care. It's a tale of financial acumen, where the medical community learned to harness the tax code to their advantage.

In "Balancing the Ledger"

We uncover the intricate dance between taxation and the medical community during the Trump administration. This chapter not only unveils the tax policies that reinstated financial equilibrium for physicians but also celebrates the transformative ripple effect they sparked within the medical community. It's a testament to the belief that when financial burdens are lifted, the healing hands of healthcare professionals can reach even greater heights of innovation, impact, and care.

"Tax Policies Under the Microscope,"

we embark on an in-depth examination of President Trump's tax policies. This meticulous exploration involves dissecting the intricate details of these policies to understand their direct impact on healthcare professionals, particularly doctors.

We examine into specific aspects of these tax policies, including: the impact of President Trump's tax policies on healthcare, doctors, and patients for each of the aspects mentioned:

1. **Tax Rate Adjustments:**
   - **Healthcare:** Lower corporate tax rates may have positively affected healthcare organizations by increasing their financial resources for investments, expansions, and technology upgrades.
   - **Doctors:** Reduced individual tax rates could have provided doctors with higher take-home pay, potentially alleviating personal financial burdens.
   - **Patients:** Lower corporate taxes might have indirectly benefited patients by enabling healthcare institutions to invest in improved facilities and services.
2. **Deductions and Credits:**
   - **Healthcare:** Enhanced deductions for healthcare investments might have encouraged healthcare organizations to modernize equipment and technologies, potentially leading to better patient care.
   - **Doctors:** Medical expense deductions could have been crucial for doctors facing high medical malpractice insurance costs or expenses related to maintaining their practices.

- **Patients:** Deductions for qualified medical expenses may have provided patients with some financial relief, especially for those with significant healthcare costs.

3. **Income Reporting:**
    - **Healthcare:** Simplified income reporting may have reduced administrative burdens for healthcare organizations, allowing them to allocate resources more efficiently.
    - **Doctors:** Streamlined reporting could have made tax compliance more manageable for doctors, freeing up time for patient care.
    - **Patients:** Simplified reporting may not have directly impacted patients but could indirectly contribute to more efficient healthcare delivery.

4. **Incentives for Investment:**
    - **Healthcare:** Tax incentives for investments might have encouraged healthcare organizations to adopt innovative technologies, enhancing the quality of care.
    - **Doctors:** Doctors could have been motivated to invest in their practices, improving patient services and expanding their medical capabilities.
    - **Patients:** Increased investments in healthcare infrastructure and technology could lead to better diagnosis and treatment options for patients.

5. **Impact on Healthcare Organizations:**
    - **Healthcare:** Tax policies influencing healthcare organizations could have had a cascading effect on individual practitioners, impacting their revenue streams and financial stability.
    - **Doctors:** Doctors working within larger healthcare organizations may have been influenced by the financial health and strategic decisions of their employers.

- **Patients:** Patients might have indirectly benefited from improved healthcare services and facilities resulting from healthcare organizations' financial stability and investments.

The impact of tax policies on healthcare, doctors, and patients is multifaceted, with potential benefits and challenges for each group. These impacts can vary based on individual circumstances, but overall, tax policies can play a pivotal role in shaping the financial landscape and the quality of healthcare delivery.

"The Financial Health of Healthcare Professionals"

"Empowering Healers: The Financial Resilience of Healthcare Professionals"

In this subsection, we pivot our gaze toward the financial health of healthcare professionals. Here, we embark on a journey that delves into how tax reforms extended a helping hand to physicians and medical practitioners, offering them fresh avenues to master their financial destinies, strategize for the future, and infuse vitality into their practices. It's a narrative of empowerment—a world where doctors are bestowed with the financial flexibility to provide nothing less than the finest care to their patients.

Strategic Financial Planning

Our exploration commences with an in-depth analysis of how tax reforms redefined the landscape of financial planning for healthcare professionals. We explore the strategies and financial planning tools that became accessible to doctors, allowing them to chart their financial courses with precision and confidence. It's a narrative of financial empowerment, where practitioners became the architects of their financial destinies.

Investment Opportunities

Here, we shift our focus to the world of investment. We investigate how tax policies created an environment ripe with investment opportunities for healthcare professionals. From tax-advantaged accounts to healthcare-focused ventures, we unveil the pathways that allowed doctors to not only secure their financial futures but also infuse vitality into their practices. It's a tale of financial empowerment, where doctors became not only healers but also astute financial architects of their own success.

Navigating the Tax Landscape

Our final exploration within this subsection navigates the practical strategies employed by healthcare professionals to optimize their financial well-being within the ever-evolving tax landscape. We unearth the wisdom and insights that empowered medical practitioners to navigate the complexities of tax codes, ensuring their financial health remained robust while they continued to serve their patients with unwavering dedication. It's a story of resilience, where doctors harnessed their financial acumen to secure their livelihoods and enhance patient care.

In "Empowering Healers," we celebrate the financial resilience of healthcare professionals—a resilience that emerged from the intersection of tax reforms and the indomitable spirit of those who dedicate their lives to healing. This subsection is a testament to the belief that when financial empowerment and healthcare intertwine, the result is a world where doctors possess the resources and flexibility to provide the highest quality care to their patients.

In *"Empowering Healers,"* we celebrate the financial resilience of healthcare professionals—a resilience that emerges from the intersection of tax reforms and the indomitable spirit of those who dedicate their lives to healing. This subsection is a testament to the belief that when financial empowerment and healthcare intertwine, the result is a world where doctors possess the resources and flexibility to provide the highest quality care to their patients. It's a narrative of empowerment, financial wisdom, and unwavering dedication to healing.

"Unpacking Trump's Tax Policies: Deciphering the Fiscal Landscape for Healthcare Professionals"

Our journey embarks on a deep dive into the intricacies of the tax policies meticulously crafted under President Trump's leadership. In this chapter, we traverse the complex terrain of tax reform, gaining profound insights into the transformations that reverberated throughout the financial realm of healthcare professionals. It's an odyssey that unravels the intricate web of tax codes, unveiling their profound and far-reaching implications on the financial lives of doctors, specialists, and the broader medical community.

Under President Trump's tax reform, healthcare professionals, particularly doctors, experienced a multifaceted impact on their financial lives and the quality of patient care. This reform reshaped the fiscal landscape in ways that extended beyond mere numbers on tax returns. It had a profound ripple effect that touched both doctors and the patients they served.

Impact on Doctors:
- *Financial Flexibility*: Trump's tax policies provided doctors with increased financial flexibility. Reduced tax rates and favorable deductions allowed physicians to retain more of their earnings,

potentially alleviating financial pressures and providing room for investments in their practices.
- **Investment Opportunities:** The reform opened doors to investment opportunities, encouraging doctors to explore tax-advantaged accounts and healthcare-focused ventures. This not only secured their financial futures but also invigorated their practices with modern technologies and improved patient care.
- **Navigating Complexity:** Doctors had to navigate the complexities of the evolving tax landscape. While the reform brought opportunities, it also demanded financial acumen to optimize their financial well-being amidst changing regulations.

Ripple Effect on Patients:
- **Improved Access:** The fiscal changes influenced healthcare organizations to invest in better facilities and technologies. Patients benefited from improved access to advanced diagnostic and treatment options, enhancing the overall quality of care.
- **Reduced Costs:** For some patients, the reform offered tax deductions for medical expenses, providing a degree of financial relief, particularly for those with substantial healthcare costs.
- **Continuity of Care:** Financially stable healthcare organizations, supported by tax incentives, could maintain services and staff, ensuring the continuity of care for patients.

Cost of Healthcare:
- **Balancing Costs:** While tax reform brought financial relief for some doctors, it also prompted discussions about the cost of healthcare. The need to balance the financial health of doctors and the affordability of care for patients became a central concern.

- ***Policy Considerations:*** Trump's tax reform underscored the intricate relationship between tax policy, the financial well-being of doctors, and the cost of healthcare. It ignited debates and policy considerations about achieving a balance that supported both healthcare professionals and patients.

In essence, Trump's tax reform acted as a catalyst for change within the healthcare ecosystem. It provided doctors with financial empowerment and opportunities for investment while simultaneously influencing the accessibility and quality of care for patients. However, it also raised important discussions about the affordability and sustainability of healthcare in the United States.

Tax Relief for Medical Practitioners"

"Tax Relief for Healers: Lightening the Fiscal Load on Medical Professionals"

Our journey commences with a dedicated exploration of the tax relief measures thoughtfully introduced during the Trump administration, crafted specifically to benefit the medical community. In this subsection, we embark on an insightful journey that unveils how these meticulously tailored policies were designed to alleviate the tax burden borne by doctors, nurses, and healthcare workers. It's a narrative steeped in the spirit of financial relief—a narrative that empowered healthcare professionals to reinvest in their practices, advance their careers, and elevate the standard of care they provided to their patients.

Easing Financial Strain

Our exploration begins with a close examination of the tax policies designed to ease the financial strain on medical practitioners. We delve into the specific deductions, credits, and tax rates that were adjusted to provide relief for doctors and nurses. It's a narrative of fiscal empowerment, where healthcare professionals found respite in the form of reduced tax burdens.

Fueling Career Advancement

Here, we shift our focus to the opportunities for career advancement that arose from these tax relief measures. We explore how reduced tax liabilities allowed medical professionals to allocate resources toward furthering their education, pursuing specialized training, or expanding their practices. It's a tale of professional growth, where doctors and nurses seized the chance to advance their careers and, in turn, enhance the quality of healthcare delivery.

Elevating Patient Care

Our journey concludes with an exploration of how tax relief measures transcended fiscal matters to influence patient care positively. We unveil the tangible impacts of these policies on the lives and well-being of patients, as healthcare professionals, unburdened by excessive tax obligations, could devote more time, resources, and expertise to providing exceptional care.

In "Tax Relief for Healers," we celebrate the thoughtful measures that lightened the fiscal load on medical professionals. It's a story of financial empowerment, career advancement, and elevated patient care—a testament to the belief that when tax policies align with the healthcare sector, the result is a world where healthcare professionals are better equipped to fulfill their noble mission of healing and caring for patients.

Incentivizing Medical Innovation

"Igniting Progress: Tax Incentives Fueling Healthcare Innovation"

In this subsection, we pivot our gaze toward the captivating intersection of taxation and medical innovation. We embark on an enlightening journey that probes the profound impact of tax incentives meticulously designed to kindle creativity and research within the healthcare industry. From the alluring world of research and development tax credits to the stimulating incentives offered to healthcare startups, we unravel the intricate mechanisms that served as catalysts, propelling medical professionals to defy boundaries and explore the outer realms of possibility. It's a tale that reveals how tax policy, in its innovative form, evolved into a formidable driving force behind transformative advancements in healthcare.

Fostering Creative Research

Our exploration begins by delving into the incentives that encouraged creative research within the healthcare sector. We uncover how tax policies, such as research and development tax credits, stimulated the imaginative minds of medical professionals. These policies not only eased financial burdens but also kindled the flames of curiosity and innovation within laboratories and research facilities. It's a narrative of scientific exploration, where tax incentives became the wind beneath the wings of groundbreaking research.

Nurturing Healthcare Startups

Here, we shift our focus to the world of healthcare startups and the tax incentives that nurtured their growth. We unveil how favorable tax policies incentivized entrepreneurs and medical professionals to embark on innovative ventures. From tax credits to deductions, these incentives provided the fertile soil for startups to germinate and thrive, ultimately contributing to the reinvigoration of the healthcare landscape. It's a tale of entrepreneurial spirit, where tax policies served as the compass guiding visionaries toward the uncharted territories of healthcare innovation.

Transformative Healthcare Advancements

Our journey culminates with a reflection on the transformative advancements that emerged from this synergy between taxation and medical innovation. We illuminate the tangible outcomes—new medical technologies, groundbreaking treatments, and improved patient care—that bore testament to the power of tax incentives as catalysts for progress. It's a story of how tax policy, when intricately woven into the fabric of healthcare, became a potent force propelling the industry into the future.

In "Igniting Progress," we celebrate the remarkable journey where tax incentives, as agents of change, fueled the fires of healthcare innovation. It's a narrative of creative research, entrepreneurial endeavor, and transformative advancements—a testament to the belief that when tax policy becomes a driving force behind healthcare innovation, the result is a world where boundaries are merely invitations to explore the limitless possibilities of progress.

Conclusion of Chapter

"Conclusion: A Taxing Legacy of Empowerment"

As we draw the curtains on our exploration of the intricate relationship between taxation and the medical community during the Trump administration, we are left with an indelible legacy—a legacy of empowerment. Throughout this chapter, we ventured into the realms of tax relief, career advancement, and transformative innovation within healthcare, all of which were catalyzed by thoughtful tax policies.

In the ever-evolving landscape of healthcare, where the weight of fiscal responsibilities often threatened to overshadow the noble art of healing, tax relief emerged as a beacon of hope. Doctors, nurses, and healthcare workers found themselves unburdened by excessive tax obligations, allowing them to reinvest in their practices, advance their careers, and elevate the standard of care they provided to their patients.

Incentivizing medical innovation became not just a policy but a spark that ignited progress. Tax incentives fueled creative research, nurtured the growth of healthcare startups, and paved the way for transformative advancements that enhanced the lives of patients and pushed the boundaries of possibility.

As we reflect on this taxing legacy of empowerment, we are reminded that tax policies, when crafted with wisdom and precision, have the power to transform industries and uplift those who dedicate their lives to the betterment of society. Within these tax codes, we find the fingerprints of progress, the echoes of innovation, and the spirit of empowerment that define an era.

As we turn the page to the next chapter, we carry forward the lessons of fiscal wisdom, innovation, and the enduring belief that, in the intricate web of American healthcare, policies have the power to shape lives, influence practices, and chart the course of medicine. The journey continues

CHAPTER 4

JUDICIAL APPOINTMENTS

"Trump's judges orchestrated the healthcare balance, harmonizing liability and patient rights. Their legacy resonates in a symphony of justice and care."

Introduction: Shaping the Legal Landscape of Healthcare

Imagine American healthcare as a vast, intricate tapestry, woven together by the threads of ethics, rights, and responsibilities. In this chapter, we're about to unravel a compelling story—a story that revolves around Trump's judicial appointments and the profound impact they had on the legal landscape of healthcare.

Picture the judicial system as the guardian of ethics and rights within this tapestry. As we venture deeper into our journey, we'll discover how these judicial nominations reached into the very heart of healthcare, affecting the very essence of medical ethics, liability, and patient rights.

Judicial Appointments: Crafting the Healthcare Legal Landscape

Our journey commences with a meticulous examination of President Trump's judicial nominations—a legacy that resonates far beyond mere selection. These appointments weren't ordinary; they were seismic choices that reverberated through the corridors of power, ultimately reshaping the terrain of healthcare-related cases. Think of them as the architects of justice, wielding the power to mold the legal framework within which doctors, nurses, and healthcare workers navigate.

In this section, we'll embark on a compelling journey that unveils the immense power and responsibility entrusted to these judicial appointees. It's a narrative that explores how their decisions, interpretations, and legal prowess became the guiding forces shaping the very foundations of healthcare ethics, liability, and patient rights. Join us as we peer behind the curtain of the judicial world and discover how it interweaves with the intricate tapestry of American healthcare.

Let's elaborate on the judicial choices that have affected healthcare, including doctors, healthcare providers, and patients:

1. **Healthcare Legislation Interpretation:** Trump's judicial appointments have played a pivotal role in interpreting healthcare legislation. Their decisions have influenced the implementation and scope of healthcare laws, impacting how doctors and healthcare providers deliver care. For example, interpretations of the Affordable Care Act (ACA) can affect the availability and affordability of healthcare services.
2. **Medical Ethics and Patient Rights:** These judges have shaped the legal framework surrounding medical ethics and patient rights. Cases involving issues such as informed consent, medical decision-making, and patient privacy have been influenced by their decisions. Doctors and healthcare providers must navigate this legal landscape, ensuring they uphold ethical standards while respecting patient rights.
3. **Liability Standards:** Judicial appointments have also had a significant impact on medical liability standards. Their interpretations of medical malpractice laws and liability thresholds affect how doctors

and healthcare providers manage risk and insurance coverage. This, in turn, can influence the cost of medical practice and the availability of healthcare services for patients.

4. **Reproductive and Women's Health:** The appointment of judges who hold views on reproductive and women's health issues has influenced the legal landscape in this area. Cases related to abortion access, contraception, and reproductive healthcare have seen shifts in legal interpretations. These decisions have far-reaching consequences for both healthcare providers and patients, particularly women.

5. **Health Insurance Coverage:** Judicial choices have played a role in determining the fate of healthcare coverage initiatives. Decisions related to Medicaid expansion, the legality of certain insurance provisions, and the role of the federal government in healthcare have all impacted the availability of insurance options for patients and the financial stability of healthcare providers.

These judicial choices have created a legal framework that directly affects the practice of medicine, the ethical considerations of healthcare professionals, the liability landscape, and patients' access to care. As healthcare providers, doctors, and patients navigate this landscape, they must remain vigilant and engaged in the political process to advocate for the healthcare outcomes they believe in and ensure that the legal system aligns with their values and priorities. It's a call to action for all stakeholders in the healthcare system to participate in shaping the destiny of American healthcare.

"Trump's Judicial Influence: Charting the Moral Terrain of Healthcare"

Step into a world where moral complexity meets medical practice, and the decisions of a few reshape the ethical landscape of healthcare. In this section, we reveal the profound influence of Trump's judicial appointments on the moral dilemmas faced by healthcare professionals.

From the delicate balance of patient consent to the heart-wrenching decisions surrounding end-of-life care, these judges hold immense sway. Their interpretations redefine the ethical framework guiding healthcare professionals.

In this section, we embark on a journey into the moral conundrums faced by healthcare providers. We uncover how judicial choices reshape their ethical compass. It's not just exploration; it's a call to action. Healthcare professionals, patients, and advocates must engage in this ethical discourse, for the decisions made within this labyrinth determine the moral core of American healthcare.

Trump's judicial appointments redefined healthcare morality by influencing key aspects of medical ethics, patient rights, and the legal framework surrounding healthcare decisions. Here's how:

1. **Interpretation of Healthcare Legislation:** These judges played a critical role in interpreting healthcare legislation, including the Affordable Care Act (ACA). Their decisions influenced the implementation and scope of healthcare laws, shaping the ethical boundaries within which healthcare professionals operate. For instance, their interpretations affected the availability and affordability of healthcare services, impacting both doctors and patients.
2. **Moral Dilemmas in Medical Ethics:** Trump's judicial choices influenced moral dilemmas faced by healthcare professionals. Cases

related to issues like patient consent, end-of-life decisions, and medical decision-making saw shifts in legal interpretations. Doctors and healthcare providers had to navigate this evolving ethical landscape, ensuring they upheld ethical standards while respecting patient rights and legal boundaries.

3. **Reproductive and Women's Health:** The appointments of judges with specific views on reproductive and women's health issues reshaped the legal landscape in this domain. Cases related to abortion access, contraception, and reproductive healthcare were influenced by these judges' decisions. These changes had far-reaching consequences for healthcare providers and patients, particularly women, impacting their moral and ethical choices.

4. **Medical Liability Standards:** Judicial choices affected medical liability standards. Their interpretations of medical malpractice laws and liability thresholds influenced how doctors and healthcare providers managed risk and insurance coverage. This had implications for the cost of medical practice and the availability of healthcare services for patients.

5. **Patient Rights and Privacy:** The judges' decisions impacted patient rights and privacy. Cases involving patient confidentiality, access to medical records, and healthcare data privacy were influenced by their interpretations. Healthcare professionals had to navigate these legal considerations while upholding ethical obligations to protect patient information and rights.

In summary, Trump's judicial appointments redefined healthcare morality by shaping the interpretation of healthcare laws, influencing moral dilemmas faced by healthcare professionals, impacting reproductive and women's health issues, affecting medical liability standards, and influencing patient rights and privacy considerations. These changes created a shifting ethical landscape within which healthcare providers must operate, emphasizing the need for ongoing ethical discourse and engagement in the legal and political processes to uphold ethical standards and patient well-being.

"Balancing Medical Liability and Patient Rights: Trump's Judicial Influence"

Imagine a tightrope suspended between two essential pillars: medical liability and patient rights. In this section, we unveil how Trump's judicial appointments serve as the hands that carefully adjust this delicate equilibrium. Visualize these appointments as architects of accountability, capable of reshaping the standards of care and the responsibilities carried by healthcare professionals.

They are the custodians of fairness within the healthcare sector, recalibrating the scales of justice that affect not only doctors but also the rights and expectations of patients. With every decision, they etch a new benchmark within the vast landscape of American healthcare—a benchmark that holds ethical, moral, and practical significance.

As we embark on Chapter 4, remember that the judiciary's rulings here aren't mere legal decisions; they are ethical compass points within a profession dedicated to healing and caring for patients. Join us on this exploration as we uncover how these decisions resonate at the very heart of a profession that strives for accountability while safeguarding the rights of those in its care. It's an invitation to delve into the intricate web of medical liability and patient rights, where the decisions made have profound implications for both healthcare professionals and those they serve.

Trump's judicial appointments significantly influenced the delicate balance between medical liability and patient rights, reshaping the standards of care and the level of responsibility healthcare professional's bear. Here are examples and explanations of how this influence played out:

1. **Medical Liability Standards:** These judges have been instrumental in interpreting and shaping medical liability standards. For instance, they have ruled on cases related to medical malpractice, determining the criteria for establishing negligence. Their decisions have affected the thresholds for medical liability, impacting the accountability of healthcare professionals. This influence has direct consequences for doctors and healthcare providers, as it affects their risk management strategies and insurance coverage.

2. **Tort Reform:** Trump-appointed judges have played a role in cases related to tort reform, advocating for limits on medical liability claims. For example, they have supported measures to cap non-economic damages in medical malpractice cases. These decisions have influenced the potential financial liability of healthcare providers and, in turn, have implications for the cost of medical practice and the availability of healthcare services for patients.

3. **Patient Informed Consent:** Judicial appointments have affected cases involving patient informed consent. Judges' interpretations have influenced the legal standards for obtaining informed consent from patients before medical procedures. This impacts how healthcare professionals communicate with patients about risks, benefits, and alternatives to treatment, ensuring that patients have a clear understanding of their medical choices.

4. **Patient Privacy and Confidentiality:** These judges have ruled on cases related to patient privacy and confidentiality, shaping the legal

framework surrounding healthcare data and medical records. Their decisions have implications for how healthcare providers handle patient information and ensure compliance with privacy regulations, safeguarding patients' rights to confidentiality.

5. **Liability in Innovative Medical Practices:** Trump-appointed judges have also influenced cases related to innovative medical practices, such as experimental treatments and medical research. Their interpretations of liability standards in these contexts have a direct impact on the ability of healthcare professionals to engage in cutting-edge medical advancements while ensuring patient safety.

In essence, these judicial appointments have recalibrated the scales of justice within the healthcare sector. Their decisions have profound implications for doctors, nurses, and healthcare providers as they navigate the legal and ethical complexities of their profession. Simultaneously, these decisions affect patient rights, shaping the expectations and protections patients have in their healthcare interactions. It's a dynamic interplay where the hands of the judiciary guide the balance between medical liability and patient rights, creating a legal landscape that significantly influences the essence of healthcare in America.

Judicial Appointments and the Healthcare Equation

In the grand symphony of American healthcare, the chapter of Trump's judicial appointments stands as a powerful movement. These judges, like skilled conductors, have orchestrated the delicate balance between medical liability and patient rights, redefining the healthcare equation.

Their decisions, from medical liability standards to patient informed consent and privacy rights, have rippled through the profession of healing. Doctors and healthcare providers have navigated this evolving terrain, while patients have found their rights safeguarded within these legal melodies.

As the curtains fall on this chapter, it is not merely a legal narrative but a testament to the profound ethical and practical impact within the expansive landscape of healthcare. It reminds us that the hands of the judiciary hold the scales, shaping the very essence of healthcare in America. It is a harmonious reminder that the pursuit of justice and patient well-being remains at the heart of the medical profession, guided by the influence of these judicial decisions.

CHAPTER 5

INTERNATIONAL HEALTHCARE COMPARISONS

"In understanding our differences lies the path to global healthcare harmony." - Unknown

Introduction:

As Dr. Emily sat in her office reviewing patient charts, she couldn't help but ponder the state of healthcare not just in her own country, but across the globe. Growing increasingly curious about how other nations approached healthcare, she decided to embark on a journey of exploration. With a desire to uncover valuable insights that could potentially inform her practice and advocacy efforts, Dr. Emily delved into the intricate web of international healthcare systems.

Section 1: Understanding Global Healthcare Models

Subsection 1: Universal Healthcare Systems

In Canada, Dr. Patel witnessed firsthand the impact of a universal healthcare system on patient outcomes. One memorable patient, Maria, had been diagnosed with a chronic condition requiring ongoing treatment. Despite her modest income, Maria never had to worry about affording her medications or doctor visits, thanks to Canada's healthcare system. Dr. Patel marveled at how such comprehensive coverage enabled patients like Maria to lead healthier, more fulfilling lives.

Subsection 2: Privatized Healthcare Systems

On a medical mission trip to the United States, Dr. Santiago encountered a starkly different healthcare reality. Meeting with patients in underserved communities, he observed the challenges many faced in accessing essential healthcare services. Without adequate insurance coverage, patients often delayed seeking care, leading to worsening health outcomes. Dr. Santiago realized the urgent need for systemic reforms to address disparities and ensure equitable access to care for all.

Section 2: Trump's Approach to Global Healthcare

Subsection 1: Diplomatic Relations and International Aid

Dr. Lee, a public health advocate, closely monitored the impact of Trump's foreign policy decisions on global health initiatives. While attending a conference on infectious diseases, she learned of funding cuts to international aid programs aimed at combatting emerging pandemics. Witnessing the tangible consequences of reduced funding, Dr. Lee became increasingly vocal in advocating for robust support for global health efforts.

Subsection 2: Trade Policies and Healthcare Accessibility

As a researcher specializing in pharmaceutical policy, Dr. Johnson studied the effects of trade agreements on healthcare accessibility. In her analysis, she uncovered how Trump's trade policies had led to increased medication costs for patients in developing countries. Through interviews with patients and healthcare providers, Dr. Johnson highlighted the real-world implications of trade negotiations on vulnerable populations, igniting conversations about the ethical considerations at play.

Section 3: Case Studies and Comparative Analysis

Subsection 1: Case Studies of Selected Countries

Dr. Chen, an international health consultant, embarked on a comparative study of healthcare systems in Germany, Japan, and the United Kingdom. Immersing herself in each country's healthcare infrastructure, she marveled at the efficiency of Germany's multipayer system, the emphasis on preventive care in Japan, and the comprehensive coverage provided by the UK's National Health Service. Through detailed case studies, Dr. Chen gleaned valuable insights into the diverse approaches to healthcare delivery worldwide.

Subsection 2: Comparative Analysis of Key Metrics

Analyzing key healthcare metrics across nations, Dr. Taylor uncovered striking disparities in healthcare outcomes. Despite spending significantly more per capita on healthcare than other high-income countries, the United States lagged behind in key indicators such as life expectancy and infant mortality rates. Dr. Taylor's comparative analysis underscored the need for comprehensive reform efforts to address systemic deficiencies and improve healthcare outcomes for all Americans.

Conclusion: Towards a Global Healthcare Agenda

Inspired by the stories and insights gleaned from her exploration of global healthcare systems, Dr. Emily emerged with a newfound sense of purpose. Armed with a deeper understanding of the interconnectedness of health systems worldwide, she was determined to advocate for policies that prioritized equity, accessibility, and affordability. As she reflected on the lessons learned and the challenges ahead, Dr. Emily remained hopeful that by working together, the global community could pave the way towards a brighter, healthier future for all.

CHAPTER 6

PERSONAL EXPERIENCES AND TESTIMONIALS

In the heart of this journey to understand why doctors and healthcare professionals should vote for President Trump, we arrive at a pivotal chapter—a chapter that embodies the essence of personal convictions and firsthand experiences. It is here that we illuminate the voices of doctors, the custodians of health, as they share their anecdotes and testimonials, providing a glimpse into their world and the reasons that led them to choose President Trump as their preferred candidate.

Think of these doctors as storytellers, each with a unique narrative to share—a tapestry of experiences, challenges, and triumphs that have shaped their perspectives. Their voices are not merely endorsements but powerful testaments to the impact of political choices on healthcare professionals and the patients they serve.

In this first part of the chapter, we delve into the personal journeys of these doctors, exploring the values, policies, and leadership qualities that resonate with them. These stories bridge the gap between the political arena and the everyday reality of healthcare, painting a vivid picture of why President Trump finds favor among a significant segment of the medical community.

Join us in this compelling exploration of personal experiences and testimonials, where the voices of doctors take center stage, offering unique insights into the intersection of healthcare and politics. As we embark on this journey, remember that these voices represent a diverse chorus within the medical profession—a chorus that echoes the belief that President Trump's leadership holds significance for healthcare in America.

A Healing Hand: Dr. Andrews' Testimonial

Dr. Sarah Andrews had always been a dedicated family physician, known for her warm bedside manner and unwavering commitment to her patients. Her medical practice nestled in a quiet, tight-knit community had flourished over the years. Patients trusted her, not just for her medical expertise but for her genuine care.

In the lead-up to the presidential election, Dr. Andrews found herself reflecting on the state of healthcare in America. She was keenly aware of the challenges and opportunities that lay ahead. As someone deeply involved in the healthcare system, she felt it was her duty to make an informed choice, both for her profession and her patients.

One evening, after a long day at the clinic, Dr. Andrews sat down with her husband, John, to discuss the upcoming election. They had differing opinions, but they always engaged in respectful, open dialogue. John, a schoolteacher, had been leaning towards one candidate, while Dr. Andrews had her reservations. She knew that her patients, her colleagues, and her community were looking to her for guidance.

The turning point came during a routine visit to a patient's home. Mrs. Thompson, a senior citizen with a heart condition, had been a patient of Dr. Andrews for years. As Dr. Andrews conducted the examination, Mrs. Thompson began discussing the upcoming election. She had been worried about potential changes in healthcare policies, and her anxiety was palpable.

Dr. Andrews listened carefully to Mrs. Thompson's concerns, realizing that they mirrored her own worries about the future of healthcare. It was in that moment, seeing the fear and vulnerability in her patient's eyes, that she decided. She would not only vote but also actively support a candidate who aligned with her values and vision for healthcare.

Over the next few weeks, Dr. Andrews joined a network of healthcare professionals who were vocal supporters of President Trump. She attended rallies, participated in discussions, and, most importantly, began sharing her reasons for choosing him as her preferred candidate.

In her testimonials, Dr. Andrews emphasized her belief in President Trump's commitment to reducing healthcare regulations and promoting medical innovation. She cited specific policies that had a positive impact on her practice, such as the reduction in administrative burdens and the support for telemedicine expansion during the pandemic.

But what resonated most with her colleagues and patients was her passion for preserving the doctor-patient relationship. Dr. Andrews spoke eloquently about her concern that excessive government interference could erode the trust and individualized care that had always been the hallmark of American medicine.

As Election Day approached, Dr. Andrews felt a sense of purpose. She knew that her voice, along with those of her fellow healthcare professionals, could make a difference. Her testimonials, grounded in her personal experiences and genuine care for her patients, served as a testament to her commitment to both her profession and her community.

In the end, Dr. Andrews' story was not just about her support for President Trump; it was about the power of personal experiences and testimonials to influence the choices of those who shape the healthcare landscape. It was a reminder that behind every policy and every vote, there were real people, real doctors, and real patients, all seeking the best possible care for themselves and their loved ones.

Conclusion for Chapter 6: Personal Experiences and Testimonials

In the tapestry of this chapter, we have woven together the voices and experiences of doctors who stand resolutely in support of President Trump. Their testimonials, like vibrant threads, illuminate the rich mosaic of perspectives within the medical community.

These doctors, guardians of health, have shared their reasons for choosing President Trump as their preferred candidate. Their narratives have resonated with passion, conviction, and a shared vision for the future of healthcare in America. They have spoken of policies that have lightened their burdens, promoted innovation, and preserved the sanctity of the doctor-patient relationship.

Yet, beyond policies, these testimonials reveal something deeper—a profound commitment to the well-being of their patients and a dedication to the principles that define the practice of medicine. These doctors, from diverse backgrounds and specialties, are united by a belief that President Trump's leadership holds significance for the healthcare landscape.

As we close this chapter, their stories linger in the air, reminding us that healthcare is not just about policies and regulations; it is about the people who dedicate their lives to healing. The personal experiences and testimonials shared here serve as a testament to the enduring influence of personal convictions and the power of voices within the medical profession.

In the chapters to come, we will continue to explore the multifaceted reasons that drive doctors and healthcare professionals to support President Trump. Their narratives, like beacons of light, guide us through the complex terrain of healthcare politics, emphasizing that at its core, this is a profession driven by the unwavering commitment to the well-being of patients and the pursuit of excellence in care.

CHAPTER 7

TRUMP'S HEALTHCARE VISION THROUGH THE LENS OF INTEGRATIVE DOCTORS

"Integrative doctors see in President Trump a catalyst for holistic healthcare, patient-centered ideals, and innovative progress."

In the intricate tapestry of American healthcare, with its diverse perspectives, our attention turns to a unique group within the medical community—integrative doctors. These healthcare practitioners have charted an exceptional course, merging conventional medicine with holistic approaches. They emphasize the interconnectedness of the mind, body, and spirit in their pursuit of wellness.

As we venture into this chapter, we embark on a voyage to comprehend why integrative doctors, with their holistic outlook, believe that President Trump holds the key to transforming healthcare. They represent a growing movement in the medical field, one that advocates for a patient-centric, holistic, and comprehensive healthcare approach.

Picture integrative doctors as forward-thinkers who envision a healthcare system that not only addresses illnesses but also fosters well-being, preventive care, and a deeper understanding of the factors influencing health. Their support for President Trump is underpinned by the belief that his leadership aligns with their values and their vision for a healthcare system that prioritizes integration and patient-centered care.

Within this chapter, we will delve into the perspectives and convictions of integrative doctors, gaining insight into the policies, principles, and leadership attributes that resonate with them. Their viewpoints offer a unique vantage point from which to examine the evolving landscape of American healthcare.

Come with us on this enlightening expedition, as we uncover why integrative doctors view President Trump as a beacon of transformation and hope—a leader they believe has the potential to guide healthcare towards a more holistic and patient-focused destination.

here are six reasons why integrative doctors believe President Trump is the answer to healthcare transformation:

"Prescription for Transformation: Why Integrative Doctors Rally Behind President Trump's Healthcare Vision"

Here are ten reasons why integrative doctors believe President Trump is the answer to healthcare transformation:

1. **Alignment with Holistic Values:** Integrative doctors emphasize holistic healthcare, focusing on the interconnectedness of physical, mental, emotional, and spiritual well-being. President Trump's recognition of the importance of mental health and wellness initiatives aligns with these values. For example, the Trump administration launched the "Every Mind Matters" campaign to promote mental health awareness and resources.
2. **Patient-Centered Care:** Integrative medicine prioritizes patient involvement in decision-making. President Trump's support for telemedicine expansion during the COVID-19 pandemic allowed patients to access care more conveniently and participate in their treatment plans, aligning with the patient-centered approach.
3. **Reducing Regulatory Barriers:** Integrative doctors advocate for fewer regulatory constraints on alternative therapies. President

Trump signed the "Right to Try" Act, allowing terminally ill patients to access experimental treatments, reducing regulatory barriers and providing patients with more choices.

4. **Preventive Care:** Integrative medicine emphasizes wellness and disease prevention. President Trump's focus on promoting healthy lifestyles and initiatives like "Be Best" for children's health align with the preventive care aspect of integrative medicine.

5. **Research and Innovation:** Integrative medicine thrives on research and innovation. President Trump's administration provided funding for research into alternative therapies like acupuncture for veterans with chronic pain, supporting innovation in healthcare.

6. **Patient Choice and Access:** Integrative doctors value diverse treatment options. President Trump's promotion of health savings accounts (HSAs) and association health plans (AHPs) empowered patients to choose healthcare plans that suited their needs, enhancing access to various treatments.

7. **Right to Try Act:** President Trump's signing of the "Right to Try" Act allowed terminally ill patients to explore experimental treatments not yet approved by the FDA. This legislation provided patients with the freedom to choose alternative therapies when facing life-threatening conditions.

8. **Reducing Healthcare Costs:** President Trump's focus on reducing drug prices and efforts to eliminate surprise medical billing align with integrative doctors' goal of making holistic treatments more affordable. Lower healthcare costs can make alternative therapies accessible to a broader range of patients.

9. **Promotion of Natural and Alternative Therapies:** The Trump administration expressed openness to natural and alternative

therapies. For example, they explored acupuncture as a potential treatment for veterans with chronic pain, recognizing the value of complementary treatments.

10. **Empowerment of Medical Professionals:** Integrative doctors believe that President Trump's policies empowered healthcare professionals to make decisions based on expertise and patient needs. Policies like expanding telemedicine and reducing administrative burdens allowed doctors to offer more personalized and holistic care.

These examples illustrate how President Trump's policies and initiatives align with the values and goals of integrative doctors, promoting holistic, patient-centered, and innovative approaches to healthcare.

"Charting the Path Forward: A Vision of Holistic Healthcare Advocated by Integrative Doctors"

In the ever-evolving landscape of American healthcare, we've embarked on a journey into the realm of integrative medicine—a world where traditional practices meet holistic wisdom, and the patient's well-being takes center stage. Throughout this chapter, we've delved into the compelling reasons why integrative doctors believe that President Trump represents the key to healthcare transformation.

As we conclude this chapter, one thing becomes abundantly clear: the voices of integrative doctors are a testament to the diverse tapestry of healthcare perspectives in our nation. Their vision for a more holistic, patient-centered, and accessible healthcare system resonates with the ideals of patient empowerment, innovative solutions, and a well-rounded approach to well-being.

In the chapters to come, we'll continue to explore the multifaceted facets of healthcare, guided by the diverse voices and perspectives that shape its future. The journey has only just begun, and the transformations ahead are as diverse as the patients we aim to serve.

So, join us as we move forward, driven by the belief that healthcare should be comprehensive, patient-centric, and ever-evolving—a belief shared by integrative doctors who see in President Trump a catalyst for a healthcare system that cares for the whole person, body and soul.

CHAPTER 8

TELEMEDICINE AND HEALTHCARE ACCESS

"Telemedicine: Bridging Gaps, Empowering All."
Transforming Healthcare. Expanding Access

Introduction:
"Connecting Care: Trump's Telemedicine Revolution"

In the realm of healthcare, distance should never stand as a barrier to quality care. Through telemedicine, we've unlocked a new era where healthcare transcends boundaries, empowers both patients and doctors, and embraces the limitless possibilities of technology. Welcome to a future where healthcare is accessible to all, regardless of where you are."

In this digital age, where technology interweaves with every facet of our lives, we delve into a chapter that explores a profound transformation in healthcare—telemedicine. As we open the pages of Chapter 8, we shine a light on President Trump's policies related to telemedicine and healthcare access, a realm where the boundaries of care have expanded beyond the traditional.

Imagine a world where a doctor's visit is just a click away, where patients can access quality care regardless of geographic barriers. This is the vision that President Trump's administration embraced—a vision where telemedicine becomes a cornerstone of healthcare accessibility and convenience.

In this chapter, we embark on a journey to understand how President Trump's policies in telemedicine have impacted doctors and patients alike. We'll witness the unfolding of a healthcare revolution, where virtual consultations, remote monitoring, and innovative technologies bridge the gap between healthcare providers and those seeking care.

Join us as we navigate this digital frontier, exploring the policies, the advancements, and the real-life stories that illuminate the path President Trump paved toward a more accessible, patient-centric healthcare system.

"Telemedicine and Healthcare Access"

In this chapter, we delve into the transformative impact of telemedicine on healthcare access during President Trump's administration. The essence of this chapter lies in the recognition of telemedicine as a revolutionary force in healthcare. It highlights how policies implemented under President Trump's leadership paved the way for a new era of healthcare delivery, one that transcends geographical barriers and prioritizes patient accessibility.

The core themes explored in this chapter include:

Telemedicine Revolution:

President Trump's administration embraced telemedicine to enhance healthcare access. The essence lies in the shift towards policies that promote the use of technology for medical consultations, prescriptions, and monitoring.

a) **Policy Embrace**: President Trump's administration recognized the potential of telemedicine as a game-changer in healthcare. They actively embraced policies that facilitated its adoption. This shift in policy focus marked a significant departure from traditional healthcare practices. The essence of this revolution lies in the recognition that telemedicine could address long-standing issues in healthcare access.

b) **Enhancing Healthcare Access**: Telemedicine represents a paradigm shift in how healthcare services are delivered. It leverages technology to bring healthcare directly into people's homes. Patients no longer need to travel long distances, face transportation barriers, or wait for extended periods to see a doctor. The essence here is the acknowledgment that telemedicine has the power to enhance healthcare access significantly.

c) **Expanding Reach**: Telemedicine extends the reach of healthcare providers. It allows doctors to connect with patients in remote or underserved areas. The essence is in the transformation of the doctor-patient relationship, where geographical constraints no longer limit access to quality care. This expansion of reach fundamentally changes how healthcare is practiced.

d) **Healthcare Beyond Boundaries**: The essence of the telemedicine revolution is in transcending physical boundaries. It envisions a healthcare system where location is no longer a barrier to receiving medical care. Patients can seek consultations, receive prescriptions, and even have their conditions monitored through digital platforms. This reshaping of healthcare's geographical constraints is at the core of the telemedicine revolution.

e) **Improving Efficiency**: Telemedicine enhances healthcare efficiency by reducing the need for in-person visits, streamlining administrative processes, and optimizing resource allocation. This efficiency contributes to cost savings and quicker healthcare delivery. The essence is in the recognition that telemedicine can make healthcare more effective and accessible.

f) **In summary, the "Telemedicine Revolution"** within Chapter 8 embodies the profound shift towards policies that leverage technology to enhance healthcare access, expand the reach of healthcare providers, and transcend geographical boundaries. It signifies a departure from traditional healthcare practices and embraces the idea that telemedicine can make healthcare more efficient, accessible, and patient-centered. This revolution is a fundamental aspect of the changing landscape of modern healthcare.

g) **Expanded Healthcare Reach:** Telemedicine's impact on healthcare access is emphasized through its ability to reach patients in remote or underserved areas. It transforms healthcare from a location-based service to a convenient, on-demand experience.

Patient-Centric Care: The chapter underscores the essence of patient-centricity by illustrating how telemedicine empowers patients to take control of their health. It provides them with timely access to healthcare services, reducing wait times and enhancing overall care experiences.

Doctor-Patient Relationships: While telemedicine offers convenience, it also explores how it can impact doctor-patient relationships. The essence lies in the balance between virtual interactions and maintaining a meaningful connection between healthcare providers and their patients.

Technological Advancements: The chapter delves into the essence of technological advancements that have facilitated telemedicine's growth, including secure communication platforms, remote monitoring devices, and digital health records.

Impact on Doctors: Investigating how these policies have influenced healthcare providers, enabling them to reach a broader patient base, streamline healthcare delivery, and adapt to the digital age.

Overall, this chapter captures the essence of a healthcare transformation where telemedicine emerges as a vital tool for improving access, convenience, and patient-centered care. It showcases the potential of technology to reshape healthcare delivery and foster innovative solutions that benefit both doctors and patients.

Embracing a New Era of Healthcare

As we draw the curtains on this chapter, we find ourselves during a compelling story—a story that captures the essence of the telemedicine revolution. It's a narrative of change, empowerment, and improved healthcare access, affecting both patients and doctors alike.

Dr. Sarah Mitchell, a dedicated family physician, found herself at a crossroads. Her rural clinic served a tight-knit community in the heart of the Midwest, but access to specialized medical care was limited. Patients often had to endure long journeys to distant cities for specialist consultations, causing added stress and financial strain.

Enter Mr. James Anderson, a retired factory worker in his late sixties, who had been struggling with a chronic heart condition. The nearest cardiologist was hours away, and the thought of another exhausting trip was daunting. That's when Dr. Mitchell decided to embrace telemedicine, a move inspired by President Trump's healthcare policies.

Dr. Mitchell enrolled in a telemedicine program that allowed her to connect with specialists virtually. Through a secure video call, she collaborated with a renowned cardiologist, Dr. Emily Sanchez, who was miles away in a major medical center. Mr. Anderson's consultation was seamless—he didn't need to leave his home.

The impact was transformative. Dr. Mitchell could provide her patients with access to top-notch specialists without the need for arduous travel. Patients like Mr. Anderson received timely consultations, and their healthcare outcomes improved. The essence of this story lies in the realization that telemedicine had brought specialty care within reach, breaking down the barriers of distance and improving the lives of patients.

But the story doesn't end there. Dr. Mitchell herself experienced a shift in her role as a physician. She became part of a collaborative network, learning from specialists, and contributing her expertise to complex cases. Telemedicine empowered her to provide more comprehensive care, and her sense of professional fulfillment soared.

In conclusion, the telemedicine revolution, driven by President Trump's policies, has ushered in a new era of healthcare access. It's a story of doctors like Dr. Mitchell and patients like Mr. Anderson, whose lives were touched by the power of technology and policy innovation. As we move forward, we'll continue to explore the multifaceted landscape of healthcare transformation, knowing that telemedicine is a cornerstone of this evolving narrative.

CHAPTER 9

DRUG PRICING AND PHARMACEUTICAL INDUSTRY

Introduction: Paving the Path to Affordable Medicines

In the intricate web of healthcare, there exists a vital thread that impacts the lives of patients, doctors, and the very essence of medical practice—the pharmaceutical industry and drug pricing. This chapter delves into the complex terrain where health, economics, and policy intersect, with President Trump's efforts to lower drug prices at the forefront.

Imagine a world where the cost of medications can be a determining factor in a patient's access to treatment, and where the influence of pharmaceutical companies extends beyond laboratories and research centers, shaping the very policies that govern healthcare. It's within this dynamic landscape that we navigate President Trump's endeavors to address the pressing issue of drug pricing and examine the reception of these efforts within the medical community.

At the heart of this chapter lies a crucial debate: the delicate balance between the need for affordable medications and the sustainability of the pharmaceutical industry. We'll explore President Trump's strategies to lower drug prices and their impact on the availability of medications for patients, as well as the perspectives of healthcare providers who bear witness to these changes.

But it's not just about policies and economics; it's a reflection of the power dynamics that influence healthcare decisions. Pharmaceutical companies, with their immense resources and innovations, wield significant influence over healthcare policy. We'll scrutinize their role in shaping the landscape of drug pricing and delve into the ethical and practical implications of this influence.

As we journey through this chapter, envision a world where patients have access to the medications they need without financial burden, where doctors can prescribe with confidence, and where the pharmaceutical industry aligns its goals with the welfare of the people it serves. It's a prescription for change, a story of challenges and opportunities, and an exploration of the intricate relationship between healthcare, economics, and policy. Welcome to Chapter 9: "Drug Pricing and Pharmaceutical Industry."

Lowering Drug Prices

In this section, we delve into President Trump's determined efforts to address the soaring costs of prescription drugs. Let's begin our journey with a story that paints a vivid picture of the issue at hand.

President Trump's Efforts

Executive Orders and Initiatives

Imagine a small-town doctor, Dr. Emily Anderson, who has been practicing medicine for over two decades. She recalls a time when she could prescribe medications without worrying about her patients struggling to afford them. However, in recent years, the rising drug prices have become a significant concern.

In response to this growing issue, President Trump took decisive action. He signed a series of executive orders and launched initiatives aimed at tackling the problem head-on. These orders covered a spectrum of strategies, from promoting price transparency to allowing the importation of cheaper drugs from abroad. The initiatives sought to create a competitive market for pharmaceuticals, ultimately driving down costs for consumers like Dr. Anderson's patients.

Impact on Drug Costs

Dr. Anderson saw the impact of President Trump's efforts firsthand. She noticed that the prices of some commonly prescribed medications began to decrease. This was particularly significant for her elderly patients who were on fixed incomes and had been struggling with the high costs of their prescriptions.

For instance, the cost of insulin, a life-saving medication for many with diabetes, became more manageable for her patients. They no longer had to make tough choices between buying groceries or their essential medications. These tangible changes in drug costs were a relief for both Dr. Anderson and her patients, as they could now focus on improving their health without the burden of exorbitant drug prices.

Reception in the Medical Community

As news of President Trump's initiatives spread across the medical community, opinions varied. Some healthcare professionals, like Dr. Anderson, welcomed the changes with open arms. They saw the potential for improved patient outcomes and reduced financial strain on their patients.

However, there were differing viewpoints within the medical community. Some voiced concerns about the potential consequences of these initiatives, such as the impact on pharmaceutical research and development. The debate within the medical community highlighted the complex nature of healthcare policy and the need for a balanced approach to addressing drug prices.

Patient Experiences

Now, let's shift our focus to the patients themselves and explore their experiences with drug pricing.

Stories of Financial Strain

Meet Sarah, a single mother of two who manages a chronic medical condition. For years, she struggled to afford the medication she needed to stay healthy. High drug prices forced her to make difficult choices, often skipping doses or rationing her medications to make them last longer. The financial strain took a toll on her well-being and quality of life.

Success Stories with Affordable Medications

Conversely, there's John, a retired veteran who relies on several prescription drugs to manage his health. He saw a positive change in his life when the prices of his medications started to decrease due to President Trump's initiatives. John's newfound ability to afford his medications meant fewer hospital visits and an improved overall quality of life.

Patient Advocacy

Sarah and John's experiences are just two examples of the countless patients who faced the challenges of high drug prices. These challenges prompted the emergence of patient advocacy groups that tirelessly fought for reform. Patients, caregivers, and advocacy organizations joined forces to push for greater transparency in drug pricing and increased access to affordable medications.

In this section, we've explored the multifaceted landscape of drug pricing, from President Trump's initiatives to the stories of patients who bore the brunt of high costs. It's a testament to the complexity of the issue and the need for a balanced approach to ensure access to essential medications while maintaining incentives for pharmaceutical innovation.

Pharmaceutical Influence

In this section, we delve into the intricate web of the pharmaceutical industry's influence on healthcare policy. Let's set the stage with a compelling narrative that illustrates the power dynamics at play.

The Power of Pharmaceutical Giants

Lobbying and Political Influence

Imagine a bustling city, where towering skyscrapers represent the corporate headquarters of pharmaceutical giants. These corporations hold immense power, not only in terms of financial resources but also through their influence on policymakers. The story begins with a glimpse into the world of pharmaceutical lobbying and political sway.

Pharmaceutical companies employ formidable lobbying efforts to shape healthcare policies that align with their interests. They have a seat at the table when healthcare reforms are discussed, often steering decisions in directions that favor their profitability. As we delve deeper, we uncover the intricate strategies these giants employ to protect their market positions and ensure favorable legislation.

Drug Pricing Strategies

Within the glass-walled boardrooms of pharmaceutical companies, executives strategize on pricing their medications. This sub-subsection delves into their pricing strategies, which often involve complex calculations and considerations.

Some drug pricing strategies aim to maximize profits, leading to high costs that burden patients and healthcare systems. These strategies have garnered public attention and sparked debates on the ethics of drug pricing. We'll explore how the pursuit of revenue sometimes conflicts with the goal of making essential medications accessible to those in need.

Research and Development Costs

The pharmaceutical industry argues that the high prices of medications are necessary to cover the substantial expenses associated with research and development (R&D). Our narrative takes us into the laboratories and clinical trials where groundbreaking drugs are born.

While R&D costs are undeniably significant, questions arise about transparency and accountability. How much of the profits are reinvested into research, and how much goes to other expenses or shareholders? We'll delve into this complex issue, shedding light on the intricacies of funding innovation while ensuring affordability.

Balancing Act

Now, let's shift our focus to the delicate balancing act that policymakers face when addressing drug pricing and pharmaceutical influence.

Innovation vs. Affordability

Picture a scale, with one side representing the need for innovation in drug development and the other side symbolizing the affordability of medications for patients. This sub-subsection explores the intricate balancing act policymakers must perform to ensure that the pharmaceutical industry thrives while patients can access vital medications without financial hardship.

We'll examine the policies and proposals aimed at striking this balance, recognizing the importance of incentivizing innovation while protecting consumers from exorbitant drug prices.

The Role of Generic Medications

Generic medications often offer a more affordable alternative to brand-name drugs. However, the pharmaceutical industry isn't passive when it comes to generics. This sub-subsection delves into the strategies employed by pharmaceutical giants to maintain their market dominance even when patents expire.

We'll explore the impact of these strategies on the availability of cost-effective generic drugs and the challenges faced by patients and healthcare systems in ensuring access to affordable alternatives.

International Drug Pricing

The world is interconnected, and drug pricing policies in one country can have ripple effects across borders. This sub-subsection investigates international drug pricing practices and their implications on global healthcare.

We'll examine how countries with different pricing approaches negotiate drug prices with pharmaceutical companies and how these negotiations can influence the affordability of medications in the United States. It's a complex dance of international policies, market forces, and pharmaceutical influence.

In this section, we've embarked on a journey through the intricate landscape of pharmaceutical influence on healthcare policy. From lobbying and pricing strategies to the delicate balance between innovation and affordability, we've illuminated the multifaceted nature of this critical issue in American healthcare.

The Quest for Affordable Medicines

In this section, we embark on a quest to understand the various efforts and solutions aimed at making medicines more affordable for all Americans. Let's set the stage with a story that illustrates the challenges faced by patients and the urgent need for affordable medications.

Patient Advocacy Movements

Grassroots Efforts

Meet Sarah, a mother of two young children diagnosed with a rare genetic disorder that requires a specialized medication. She becomes the face of a grassroots patient advocacy movement, driven by the dire need for affordable access to life-saving drugs.

Sarah's journey leads her to connect with other families facing similar struggles. Together, they organize rallies, share personal stories, and raise their voices to demand change. Sarah's story shines a light on the power of patient advocacy movements in raising awareness about the critical issue of drug affordability.

Policy Recommendations

Dr. Johnson, a healthcare policy expert, enters the narrative with a comprehensive understanding of the legislative landscape.

He outlines a series of policy recommendations that could address the soaring costs of medications in the United States. Dr. Johnson's insights highlight the potential for regulatory reforms to create a more affordable pharmaceutical market.

From importation measures to patent reform, these policy recommendations become a focal point for policymakers and advocates seeking to reduce the financial burden on patients and healthcare systems.

Access to Essential Medications

As we explore further, we encounter Maria, a nurse dedicated to caring for patients with chronic illnesses. She sheds light on the challenges patients face in accessing essential medications due to high costs and insurance limitations.

Maria's perspective emphasizes the critical importance of ensuring access to life-saving drugs for all patients, irrespective of their financial circumstances. Her story drives the discussion about the ethical dimensions of drug pricing and the need to prioritize access as a fundamental healthcare right.

Envisioning Tomorrow's Solutions

Now, we shift our focus to the future, where potential solutions and innovations offer hope for more affordable medicines.

Legislative Reforms

John, a seasoned lawmaker, shares his commitment to driving legislative reforms aimed at lowering drug prices. He discusses bills and initiatives designed to increase transparency, promote competition, and hold pharmaceutical companies accountable.

John's perspective offers insights into the legislative path forward, showcasing how policymakers are actively seeking solutions to address the affordability crisis in healthcare.

The Role of Technology

In our final sub-subsection, we meet Emily, a tech entrepreneur passionate about leveraging innovation to make healthcare more accessible. She introduces us to cutting-edge technologies, such as telemedicine, prescription price comparison tools, and digital health platforms.

Emily's vision illustrates how technology can empower patients to make informed decisions about their healthcare and navigate the complex landscape of drug pricing. Her story sparks a discussion on the transformative potential of technology in enhancing medication affordability and accessibility.

In this section, we've embarked on a journey to understand the quest for affordable medicines, from grassroots patient advocacy movements to policy recommendations and the promising role of technology. Through the stories of individuals like Sarah, Dr. Johnson, Maria, John, and Emily, we explore the multifaceted efforts to tackle the challenge of drug affordability and envision a future where essential medications are within reach for all Americans.

Navigating the Future of Healthcare Transformation in the Era of Trumpism

In the ever-evolving landscape of healthcare, the chapter on drug pricing and the pharmaceutical industry unraveled a complex tapestry of challenges, hopes, and innovations. It was a chapter marked by the profound influence of pharmaceutical giants, the quest for affordable medicines, and the tireless advocacy of patients and healthcare professionals.

As we conclude this chapter, we find ourselves at a crossroads—a juncture where the healthcare industry grapples with the delicate balance between innovation and affordability. The efforts of the Trump administration to lower drug prices have sparked debates, sparked conversations, and, in some cases, ignited a ray of hope for those burdened by the high cost of medications.

Through the lens of patient advocacy movements, we witnessed the power of grassroots efforts and the emergence of policy recommendations aimed at ensuring access to essential medications for all. These voices, driven by the very real experiences of patients, remind us that the pursuit of affordable healthcare is a collective responsibility.

Looking ahead, we envision tomorrow's solutions, exploring the potential for legislative reforms to reshape the drug pricing landscape and the role of technology in facilitating access to medications. It is a future filled with possibilities—a future where the right to affordable medicines is not a distant dream but a tangible reality.

As we move forward in our exploration of healthcare transformation, let us carry with us the lessons learned from this chapter—a chapter that reminds us of the critical importance of balancing innovation with accessibility, and the undeniable power of advocacy in shaping the healthcare policies of tomorrow.

CHAPTER 10

MENTAL HEALTH AND VETERANS' CARE

Mental Health Initiatives

In this section, we delve into the initiatives undertaken by the Trump administration to address the critical issue of mental health. These initiatives were not only aimed at improving the mental well-being of Americans but also had a significant impact on healthcare workers who were on the frontline of providing mental health services.

Presidential Task Force on Mental Health

Within this subsection, we explore the creation and objectives of the Presidential Task Force on Mental Health, a pivotal initiative that shaped the mental health landscape during President Trump's tenure. We examine how this task force came into existence, its overarching objectives, and its composition, which included key members from various federal agencies. This sub-subsection provides insight into the strategic approach taken by the Trump administration to address mental health on a national scale.

The Interagency Working Group

Continuing our exploration, we delve into the Interagency Working Group, an integral component of the Presidential Task Force on Mental Health. We discuss how this collaborative effort brought together experts from diverse fields and agencies to work collectively towards improving mental health services. This sub-

subsection highlights the synergy between different branches of the government and professionals in the mental health field, emphasizing their shared commitment to advancing mental healthcare.

Improving Access to Mental Health Services

In the final part of this subsection, we investigate the efforts made to enhance access to mental health services. This includes policies and programs aimed at reducing barriers to mental healthcare, expanding the availability of services, and increasing awareness about mental health issues. We also explore how these initiatives impacted healthcare workers, who played a vital role in delivering mental health services to those in need.

Veteran Suicide Prevention

Moving forward, we shift our focus to veteran suicide prevention, a critical aspect of mental health initiatives that directly affected healthcare workers and veterans alike.

The PREVENTS Initiative

Within this sub-subsection, we explore the groundbreaking PREVENTS (President's Roadmap to Empower Veterans and End a National Tragedy of Suicide) Initiative. We discuss its inception, its multifaceted approach to preventing veteran suicide, and the collaborative efforts involving healthcare workers, veterans, and various stakeholders. This sub-subsection sheds light on the profound impact of the PREVENTS Initiative on the mental health landscape, particularly in the context of veterans' care.

Expanding Mental Health Support

Continuing our exploration, we delve into the expansion of mental health support for veterans. This includes the implementation of programs and resources aimed at providing comprehensive mental health care to those who have served in the military. We also examine the role of healthcare workers in delivering these services and the challenges they faced in addressing the unique mental health needs of veterans.

Crisis Line and Outreach Programs

In the final part of this section, we discuss the crisis lines and outreach programs established to provide immediate assistance and support to veterans in crisis. We highlight the pivotal role played by healthcare workers in operating these programs and ensuring that veterans receive timely and effective mental health care.

Overall, This Section provides an in-depth look at the mental health initiatives undertaken during the Trump administration and their impact on healthcare workers and veterans. It sets the stage for a comprehensive exploration of mental health and veterans' care in the following subsections, offering a nuanced perspective on the evolving landscape of mental healthcare in the United States.

Impact on Healthcare Workers

In this section, we delve into the profound impact of the Trump administration's initiatives on healthcare workers who are at the forefront of providing care to veterans. These initiatives not only aimed to improve veterans' access to healthcare but also recognized and supported the crucial role played by healthcare workers.

Supporting Veterans' Caregivers

Within this subsection, we explore the various ways in which the Trump administration supported caregivers of veterans, including training and resources, recognition of their role, and the introduction of the VA MISSION Act.

Training and Resources

We begin by examining the training and resources made available to veterans' caregivers. This includes educational programs and support networks designed to equip caregivers with the knowledge and skills needed to provide effective care to veterans. We delve into the impact of these resources on healthcare workers who often collaborate closely with caregivers to ensure the well-being of veterans.

Recognizing the Role of Caregivers

Continuing our exploration, we discuss the recognition of the vital role played by caregivers in the care of veterans. We examine policies and initiatives that aimed to acknowledge and support caregivers as essential members of the healthcare team. We also highlight the experiences of healthcare workers who collaborated with caregivers to enhance veterans' care.

The VA MISSION Act

In the final part of this subsection, we delve into the VA MISSION (Maintaining Internal Systems and Strengthening Integrated Outside Networks) Act, a landmark legislation that sought to improve veterans' access to healthcare services. We explore how this act impacted healthcare workers, including their roles in implementing its provisions and its influence on veterans' care.

Veterans' Mental Health Training for Healthcare Professionals

Moving forward, we shift our focus to the training of healthcare professionals in veterans' mental health care, an essential aspect of veterans' healthcare.

Expanding Education

Within this sub-subsection, we explore the expansion of education and training programs aimed at equipping healthcare professionals with the knowledge and skills required to address veterans' mental health needs. We discuss the impact of these programs on healthcare workers and their ability to provide specialized care to veterans.

Bridging the Gap

Continuing our exploration, we delve into efforts to bridge the gap between veterans' mental health care and general healthcare services. We examine how healthcare workers played a pivotal role in ensuring seamless access to mental health care for veterans and the challenges they faced in this process.

Stories from Healthcare Workers

In the final part of this section, we share stories and experiences from healthcare workers who provided mental health care to veterans. These narratives provide a firsthand account of the challenges, successes, and profound impact of healthcare workers in veterans' mental health care.

Overall, this Section sheds light on the transformative impact of the Trump administration's initiatives on healthcare workers involved in veterans' care. It highlights the recognition of caregivers, the training of healthcare professionals, and the experiences of those on the frontlines, offering a comprehensive perspective on the evolving landscape of veterans' healthcare in the United States.

The Road Ahead

In this section, we embark on a journey that explores the path ahead in the realm of mental health and veterans' care. We delve into both the ongoing challenges that persist and the promising prospects that offer hope and transformation.

Ongoing Challenges
Addressing Stigma

The first part of this subsection delves into the persistent challenge of addressing stigma surrounding mental health issues, particularly within the veteran community. We examine the efforts required to change perceptions and promote open conversations about mental health. Healthcare workers play a critical role in combatting stigma, and we explore their experiences and insights in this context.

Expanding Access

Continuing our exploration, we discuss the ongoing challenge of expanding access to mental health services for veterans. Despite progress, there remain barriers to access that affect veterans and their families. Healthcare workers continue to work diligently to overcome these challenges, and we highlight their efforts and innovative solutions.

Integrating Mental Health into Primary Care

In the final part of this subsection, we delve into the ongoing work of integrating mental health care into primary care settings. This represents a critical step in providing comprehensive care to veterans. We explore the experiences and perspectives of healthcare workers who are at the forefront of this integration, highlighting the importance of a holistic approach to veterans' well-being.

Future Predictions

Legislative Reforms

Within this part of the chapter, we explore potential legislative reforms that hold promise for the future of mental health and veterans' care. We discuss how policymakers, healthcare workers, and veterans themselves advocate for changes in legislation that can enhance the quality and accessibility of mental health services.

Leveraging Telehealth

Continuing our exploration, we delve into the role of telehealth in shaping the future of mental health care for veterans. Telehealth has emerged as a powerful tool, particularly in providing remote and timely support. We discuss how healthcare workers are leveraging telehealth solutions to bridge gaps in care and improve veterans' access to mental health services.

The Role of Community Support

In the final part of this section, we focus on the critical role of community support in veterans' mental health and overall well-being. We explore how community-based initiatives and organizations collaborate with healthcare workers to provide holistic care to veterans. We also share stories of healthcare workers and community members working together to create a supportive environment for veterans.

"The Road Ahead,"

Offers a comprehensive perspective on the challenges and opportunities in the field of mental health and veterans' care. It sheds light on the ongoing efforts to address stigma, expand access, and integrate mental health into primary care, while also exploring legislative reforms, the potential of telehealth, and the vital role of community support in shaping the future landscape of care for veterans.

Navigating the Future of Mental Health and Veterans' Care

As we conclude Chapter 10, "Mental Health and Veterans' Care," it's fitting to encapsulate the essence of our journey with a poignant story that resonates with the heart of this chapter.

In the heart of a bustling city, we meet John, a decorated veteran who had carried the weight of his experiences long after his service. For years, he grappled with the invisible scars of combat, often shying away from seeking help due to the stigma surrounding mental health. His path was fraught with challenges, but hope emerged in an unexpected place—his community clinic.

John's journey toward healing was guided by compassionate healthcare workers who understood the unique struggles veterans like him faced. Through dedicated programs, they provided mental health support that was seamlessly integrated into his primary care visits. With every session, John found solace in sharing his experiences, and the stigma began to dissipate.

But it wasn't just within the clinic walls that change was happening. In his community, support groups and initiatives rallied around veterans, offering a network of understanding and companionship. Healthcare workers, community leaders, and volunteers joined forces, realizing that the journey toward mental health and well-being was a collective effort.

John's story is not unique. It's a testament to the tireless dedication of healthcare workers who continue to break down barriers, the resilience of veterans who seek help, and the strength of communities that stand together. This chapter has illuminated the initiatives, challenges, and triumphs that define mental health and veterans' care under the influence of President Trump.

As we move forward, let us remember that the road ahead is one of continuous improvement, marked by legislative reforms, telehealth innovations, and the unwavering support of communities. Together, we can ensure that every veteran, like John, finds the healing and care they deserve.

Chapter 10 has been a testament to the power of compassion, resilience, and collective action. It has shown us that, as a nation, we are committed to honoring our veterans and providing them with the mental health care they need. In the chapters that follow, we will continue to explore the evolving landscape of healthcare and the transformative impact of leadership on the well-being of our citizens.

CHAPTER 11

PUBLIC HEALTH AND THE PANDEMIC

Navigating the Storm

The Early Days - A Race Against the Unknown

In the early days of the COVID-19 pandemic, the world found itself grappling with an invisible enemy, a virus that threatened lives and challenged the very foundations of public health. On the frontlines of this crisis were healthcare professionals, who faced an unprecedented challenge.

Dr. Emily's Call to Action

Dr. Emily, an infectious disease specialist in New York City, vividly recalls the initial response to the pandemic. Hospitals were inundated, and medical supplies were scarce. In those early days, healthcare workers faced a daunting task: how to contain the virus while protecting their own safety. Dr. Emily, along with her colleagues, worked tirelessly to adapt to the evolving situation. They improvised personal protective equipment, developed triage protocols, and shared critical information with colleagues around the world. It was a race against the unknown, and healthcare professionals like Dr. Emily exemplified resilience and determination.

The Strategies That Emerged

In response to the rapid spread of COVID-19, governments and healthcare organizations implemented a range of strategies. These included lockdowns and social distancing measures to curb transmission, mask mandates, and travel restrictions. Health agencies like the CDC provided guidelines for testing, isolation, and contact tracing.

The Search for Solutions - Vaccine Development and Testing

As the pandemic raged on, the urgent need for a vaccine became evident. Governments, pharmaceutical companies, and researchers worldwide embarked on a mission to develop safe and effective vaccines at an unprecedented pace.

Operation Warp Speed

Operation Warp Speed, a U.S. government initiative, aimed to accelerate vaccine development and distribution. Dr. Sarah, a vaccinologist, was part of the team that worked tirelessly to bring a vaccine to the public. The initiative prioritized funding streamlined regulatory processes, and forged partnerships between pharmaceutical companies and research institutions. Dr. Sarah and her colleagues faced immense pressure to maintain rigorous safety standards while expediting the vaccine timeline.

Testing and Tracing at Scale

Efforts to combat the pandemic also involved ramping up testing and contact tracing. In communities across the country, healthcare workers and volunteers joined forces to conduct mass testing, ensuring that individuals with the virus were identified and isolated.

Through these stories, Subsection 1 and Subsection 2 illuminate the early response to the pandemic, the strategies employed to mitigate its impact, and the immense challenges faced by healthcare professionals. It underscores the dedication and innovation within the healthcare community, as well as the urgency of finding solutions in the face of a global crisis.

The Healthcare Community's Perspective

Voices from the Frontlines - Battling the Unseen Foe

As the COVID-19 pandemic unfolded, healthcare workers found themselves thrust into a battle unlike any they had faced before. Their experiences on the frontlines were marked by sacrifice, resilience, and an unwavering commitment to saving lives.

A Nurse's Tale

Nurse James, working in a busy urban hospital, faced the full force of the pandemic's impact. He vividly recounts the harrowing experiences of caring for critically ill patients, often with limited resources. The emotional toll on healthcare workers like Nurse James was immense, as they had to navigate the complexities of providing care while coping with their own fears and anxieties.

Triumph Amidst Adversity

On a brighter note, Subsection 1 also features stories of triumph. Dr. Maria, an ER physician, shares her account of successfully treating patients and witnessing their recovery. She highlights the moments of hope and resilience that emerged during adversity, showcasing the unwavering spirit of healthcare professionals.

Subsection 2: Public Health Policies Through the Eyes of Professionals - Insights and Contention

The government's response to the pandemic drew both praise and criticism from healthcare experts. Subsection 2 delves into the perspectives of these professionals, shedding light on their views and insights.

Finding Common Ground

Dr. Laura, a public health expert, emphasizes the importance of evidence-based policies and collaborative efforts between government agencies and healthcare professionals. Her view represents a consensus within the healthcare community on the need for a coordinated response to the pandemic.

Contending Perspectives

However, Subsection 2 also explores areas of contention within the healthcare community. Dr. Michael, an epidemiologist, expresses concern about the consistency and transparency of public health messaging. He believes that clearer communication could have mitigated confusion and led to more effective public compliance with safety measures.

Through these stories, Subsection 1 and Subsection 2 provide a comprehensive view of the healthcare community's perspective on the pandemic. It highlights the sacrifices and challenges faced by healthcare workers, as well as the diversity of opinions within the field regarding government policies and responses. The section offers valuable insights into the collective experiences and wisdom of those at the forefront of battling the pandemic.

Lessons Learned and the Path Forward

Reflections and Accountability - Navigating Successes and Failures

In the wake of the COVID-19 pandemic, Subsection 1 invites us to reflect on the successes and failures of the healthcare response, emphasizing the need for transparency and accountability.

Celebrating Triumphs

Dr. Sarah, an infectious disease specialist, shares her perspective on the triumphs achieved in vaccine development. She highlights the remarkable scientific collaboration that led to vaccine breakthroughs in record time. Dr. Sarah underscores the significance of these achievements in preventing further loss of life.

Calls for Accountability.

Subsection 1 also delves into the critical topic of accountability. Nurse Emily advocates for transparency in reporting COVID-19 data. She recounts instances where inconsistent reporting affected decision-making and hindered effective responses. Her story underscores the importance of accountability in healthcare systems.

Preparing for Future Crises - Strategies for Resilience

This Subsection explores strategies and policies proposed for better pandemic preparedness and analyzes the valuable lessons that can be applied to future public health challenges.

Building Resilience

Dr. Carlos, a public health strategist, outlines his vision for building resilience in the face of future pandemics. He emphasizes the need for long-term investments in healthcare infrastructure, bolstering research capabilities, and fostering international collaboration. Dr. Carlos's insights offer a roadmap for policymakers and healthcare leaders.

Applying Lessons Beyond COVID-19

Finally, Subsection 2 concludes with a story from Dr. Maya, a community health advocate. She reflects on how the lessons learned from the COVID-19 pandemic can be applied to other public health challenges, such as climate-related health crises. Dr. Maya's perspective highlights the interconnectedness of health issues and the importance of a holistic approach to healthcare.

Through these stories, Section 3 provides a nuanced exploration of the pandemic's impact, both in terms of successes and areas for improvement. It calls for transparency and accountability while offering a roadmap for better pandemic preparedness and the application of lessons learned to future public health challenges. It serves as a testament to the resilience and adaptability of healthcare professionals in the face of unprecedented challenges.

Conclusion: "Resilience in Adversity: A Test of Our Healthcare System"

In the tumultuous landscape of a global pandemic, Chapter 11 serves as a poignant reflection on the healthcare response to the COVID-19 crisis during the Trump administration. It is a chapter marked by resilience, innovation, and the unwavering commitment of healthcare professionals.

As we conclude this chapter, it is evident that the COVID-19 pandemic was a litmus test of our healthcare system. It revealed the strengths, weaknesses, and, above all, the resilience of the healthcare community. In the face of unprecedented challenges, doctors, nurses, public health experts, and countless others demonstrated their dedication to saving lives.

From the early days of uncertainty to the development and distribution of vaccines, we witnessed stories of triumph and calls for accountability. Voices from the frontlines echoed with tales of heroism, sacrifice, and the relentless pursuit of providing the best care possible.
Our exploration of public health policies through the eyes of healthcare professionals revealed a diverse range of views and opinions. It showcased the complexity of managing a crisis of this magnitude and highlighted areas of consensus and contention.

In the final section, "Lessons Learned and the Path Forward," we listened to reflections on successes and failures and recognized the urgent need for transparency and accountability in healthcare systems. We explored strategies for better pandemic preparedness and the application of invaluable lessons to future public health challenges.

This chapter encapsulates a pivotal moment in healthcare history—a moment that challenged our collective resilience and determination. It is a testament to the enduring spirit of healthcare professionals and their unwavering commitment to the well-being of individuals and communities.

As we move forward in our journey through the intricate web of American healthcare, let the lessons from this chapter serve as a reminder of the remarkable capacity of the healthcare system to adapt, learn, and ultimately, to heal. The pandemic may have tested us, but it has also strengthened our resolve to meet future challenges head-on, with compassion, innovation, and a dedication to the principles that underpin the noble art of healing.

CHAPTER 12

MEDICAL EDUCATION AND RESEARCH FUNDING

"Building the Future of Medicine"

In the ever-evolving world of healthcare, where innovation and progress are the lifeblood of medical advancements, Chapter 12 takes us on a journey into the realms of medical education and research funding. Here, we explore the critical policies put forth during the Trump administration that have a profound impact on the future of the medical profession.

Imagine this chapter as a bridge—a bridge that connects the past, present, and future of medicine. It is a chapter that underscores the importance of nurturing the minds and talents of aspiring healthcare professionals and fueling the engines of medical discovery. It's a testament to the belief that investment in medical education and research is an investment in the health and well-being of future generations.

As we delve into this chapter, we will closely examine the policies that shaped medical education, from student loans to workforce development initiatives. We will also unravel the intricate web of research funding, from NIH budgets to groundbreaking research initiatives. These policies, rooted in the belief that knowledge is the cornerstone of medical progress, have set the stage for a future where healthcare is poised for remarkable transformation.

Join us on this enlightening journey as we discover how President Trump's administration steered the ship of medical education and research funding. Their influence is etched into the very foundations of our healthcare system, shaping the physicians, researchers, and innovations that will define the future of medicine.

Building the Future of Medicine

In the complex tapestry of healthcare, the threads of medical education and research funding weave a future that holds the promise of innovation, progress, and excellence. As we delve into Chapter 12, we embark on a journey to explore how the policies and initiatives of the Trump administration sculpted the landscape for future healthcare professionals and researchers. This chapter illuminates the pivotal role that education and research funding play in shaping the future of medicine.

Nurturing the Future Generation

Medical Education Policies

In the first subsection, we navigate through the transformative reforms in medical education policies under President Trump's leadership. Here, we explore how these changes have influenced aspiring healthcare professionals and the medical schools that train them. Through real-life stories, we unveil the impact of these policies on the journey of medical students.

1. ***Student Loan Reforms:*** The burden of student loans has long haunted aspiring doctors. We delve into the stories of medical students who experienced the weight of debt and how policy changes brought relief and hope, allowing them to focus on their calling.

- *Emma's Story*: Emma, a passionate medical student, found herself drowning in student loan debt. With reforms, she discovered a path towards financial stability, enabling her to pursue her dream of becoming a pediatrician.

2. **Workforce Development Initiatives**: The healthcare workforce is the backbone of the medical profession. We uncover how workforce development initiatives impacted the training and preparation of future healthcare professionals.
    - *James' Journey*: James, an aspiring nurse, witnessed how workforce development initiatives opened doors for better training and resources. His experience showcases the positive ripple effect on the quality of care provided to patients.
3. **Expanding Medical School Capacity**: Medical school capacity directly influences the number of new doctors entering the healthcare system. Through real-life stories, we explore the expansion of medical school capacity and its impact on aspiring doctors.
    - *Maria's Aspiration*: Maria, an aspiring physician from an underserved community, shares her journey of becoming a medical student thanks to the expansion of local medical school capacity. Her story reflects the administration's commitment to addressing healthcare disparities.

The Impact on Aspiring Healthcare Professionals

In the second subsection, we shift our focus to the experiences of aspiring healthcare professionals. Through their testimonials, we gain insights into the challenges they face, including the evolving landscape of medical school admissions.

1. **Student Testimonials**: *Balancing Debt and Dreams*: Aspiring healthcare professionals, with their dreams of healing and caring for pa-

tients, often grapple with the financial realities of their education. We hear from students who have walked this tightrope, balancing their passion for medicine with the burden of student loans.

- ○ ***David's Dilemma:*** David, a dedicated medical student, shares his experiences of balancing his dream of becoming a surgeon with the financial challenges of medical school. His journey epitomizes the resilience of those committed to the medical profession.

2. ***The Changing Landscape*** *of Medical School Admissions*: Medical school admissions are evolving to embrace a more diverse pool of applicants. We explore the changing dynamics of medical school admissions and its implications for the future of healthcare professionals.

- ○ ***Lila's Ascent:*** Lila, a trailblazing medical school applicant from a non-traditional background, shares her path to becoming a medical student, emphasizing the importance of inclusivity in shaping the future of medicine.

In this section, we immerse ourselves in the narratives of aspiring healthcare professionals, understanding how policy reforms have shaped their journeys and aspirations, setting the stage for a brighter and more diverse future in medicine.

CHAPTER 13

ETHICS IN HEALTHCARE

Navigating the Moral Compass of Medicine

In the complex world of healthcare, where life and well-being hang in the balance, ethics serve as the guiding stars that illuminate the path. Chapter 13 delves into the intricate realm of medical ethics and how they intertwine with the policies and decisions made during President Trump's tenure.

As we embark on this journey, we'll navigate the moral compass of medicine, exploring the fundamental principles and ethical dilemmas that healthcare professionals face daily. From patient autonomy to resource allocation, ethics lie at the heart of every healthcare decision.

Our exploration begins by dissecting the ethical considerations embedded within President Trump's policies. We'll scrutinize how these policies impacted the delicate balance between patient rights, healthcare access, and affordability. The goal is to unravel the ethical implications, both intended and unintended, of these policy choices.

However, the terrain of medical ethics is far from monolithic. Controversies, debates, and ethical quandaries often divide the medical community. We'll dive headfirst into these debates, shedding light on issues such as physician-assisted suicide, organ transplantation ethics, and the role of conscience clauses in healthcare.

Through the lens of real-life stories, we'll confront these ethical dilemmas head-on. From the perspectives of patients, families, and healthcare providers, we'll understand the profound impact of ethical decisions on lives and well-being.

Chapter 13 is an odyssey into the complex and ever-evolving world of medical ethics. It is a journey that challenges our understanding of right and wrong, explores the gray areas of medical decision-making, and underscores the importance of ethics as the cornerstone of compassionate and principled healthcare. Join us as we navigate the moral landscape that.

Navigating the Moral Compass of Medicine

In the bustling halls of a modern hospital, Dr. Sarah found herself at a crossroads. She had always believed in the sanctity of her profession, but the decisions she faced now were morally complex. As she grappled with these ethical dilemmas, she couldn't help but reflect on the long history of medical ethics, dating back to ancient Greece. The story of Hippocrates and his Oath, a solemn promise to prioritize patients' well-being above all else, resonated with her. Dr. Sarah realized that understanding the historical roots of medical ethics was crucial in navigating the intricate landscape of contemporary medicine.

The Foundation of Medical Ethics

Historical Perspectives

Hippocratic Oath

Dr. James had always been intrigued by the Hippocratic Oath. He often recounted the story of Dr. Maria, a physician from ancient

Greece. Dr. Maria's commitment to the Oath was unwavering. She once refused a wealthy patient who sought to jump the queue, ensuring that the most vulnerable received care first. Dr. James used this story to emphasize how the Hippocratic Oath's principles of compassion and justice continue to guide modern medical.

Evolution of Medical Ethics

In the small town of Merryville, Nurse Emma discovered a dusty, old medical journal from the early 20th century. She was captivated by the evolution of medical ethics over the decades. The stories within those pages revealed how ethical standards had adapted to accommodate the ever-changing landscape of healthcare. From the debates surrounding organ transplantation to the ethical challenges posed by the AIDS epidemic, Nurse Emma learned that medical ethics were not stagnant but responsive to the needs and values of society.

Autonomy

Dr. Patel recalled the story of a patient, Sarah, who had been diagnosed with a life-altering condition. Sarah's unwavering desire to be informed about her treatment options and make decisions about her own body epitomized the principle of autonomy. Dr. Patel emphasized how respecting a patient's autonomy, just as he did with Sarah, was fundamental to ethical medical practice.

Beneficence

Nurse Ramirez remembered a young boy named David, whose family struggled to afford medical care. The hospital's social worker had connected the family with a charity program, ensuring that David received the treatment he desperately needed. Nurse

Ramirez highlighted the principle of beneficence, showcasing how healthcare professionals often go above and beyond to benefit their patients.

Non-Maleficence

In the heart of the city, Dr. Jackson shared the story of a surgical team that had made a critical error during a procedure. They had inadvertently harmed a patient, and the guilt weighed heavily on their shoulders. Dr. Jackson discussed how the principle of non-maleficence emphasized the duty to do no harm, and how healthcare providers must always strive to minimize harm to their patients.

Justice

In a bustling urban clinic, Nurse Roberts worked with a diverse patient population. She remembered the story of a homeless man who had been denied medical care at another facility. Nurse Roberts was determined to ensure that everyone, regardless of their background, received equitable healthcare. She saw this as a practical application of the principle of justice in medicine – ensuring fairness and equal access to healthcare services.

This elaborate storytelling approach provides a vivid and relatable context for understanding the foundations of medical ethics, making it more engaging and relatable for readers.

Medical Ethics in Practice

As the early morning sunbathed the hospital room in a soft glow, Dr. Anderson found himself standing beside Mr. Roberts, a patient battling a severe illness. This poignant moment encapsulated the essence of medical ethics in practice. Dr. Anderson had to navigate complex decisions while upholding the principles that underpinned his profession. The stories that follow shed light on two critical aspects of medical ethics: informed consent and end-of-life ethics.

Informed Consent

Importance and Components

In a quiet examination room, Dr. Emily shared the story of Emily, a young woman facing a life-altering surgery. Dr. Emily emphasized the significance of informed consent as she explained how Emily's thorough understanding of the procedure's risks and benefits played a pivotal role in her decision-making. Dr. Emily described how she took the time to ensure that Emily was fully informed, respecting her autonomy and adhering to the ethical principle of informed consent.

Challenges and Legal Implications

In a bustling legal office, Attorney Harris recounted a challenging case involving a patient, John, who claimed he had not been adequately informed about the risks of a medical procedure. The legal battle that ensued highlighted the complex nature of informed consent and the legal implications it carried. Attorney Harris discussed how ensuring proper documentation and communication were vital not only for ethical practice but also for legal protection.

End-of-Life Ethics

DNR Orders and Advanced Directives

Nurse Rodriguez remembered the family meeting where they discussed implementing a Do-Not-Resuscitate (DNR) order for Mrs. Johnson, a terminally ill patient. The family's emotional journey was a poignant example of end-of-life ethics. Nurse Rodriguez explained the importance of respecting a patient's advance directives, enabling them to make decisions about their care even when they could no longer communicate. It was a testament to the principle of autonomy, even in the most challenging circumstances.

Euthanasia and Physician-Assisted Suicide

In a philosophical classroom, Professor Martinez engaged her students in a lively debate on the ethical aspects of euthanasia and physician-assisted suicide. She presented the story of Mr. Thompson, a patient suffering from unbearable pain due to a terminal illness. Professor Martinez explored the ethical complexities surrounding the choice to end one's life in the face of immense suffering. The debate highlighted the diverse perspectives within the medical community and society, illustrating the ongoing discussions on end-of-life ethics.

These stories bring to life the practical application of medical ethics, showcasing the challenges, dilemmas, and profound decisions that healthcare professionals encounter in their daily practice.:

Contemporary Ethical Issues

Dr. Walker stared at the MRI scan on his computer screen, analyzing the intricate details of a patient's brain. The introduction of cutting-edge technologies like artificial intelligence and genomic medicine had ushered in a new era of medical practice. However, these advances also raised ethical questions that required careful consideration. The stories below illustrate the challenges and opportunities presented by emerging technologies and the ethical complexities surrounding healthcare disparities.

Emerging Technologies

Artificial Intelligence in Medicine

In a bustling hospital, Dr. Patel shared her experience with AI-assisted diagnostics. She recounted the story of a patient whose rare condition was detected by an AI algorithm before it became life-threatening. Dr. Patel emphasized the ethical imperative of leveraging AI for patient benefit while maintaining transparency and accountability in its use. The narrative underscored the promise of AI in healthcare while highlighting the need for ethical guidelines.

Genomic Medicine and Genetic Ethics

In a genetics clinic, Genetic Counselor Davis met with a couple grappling with a difficult decision. They were considering genetic testing to assess their unborn child's risk of inheriting a rare genetic disorder. Davis explained the ethical considerations surrounding genomic medicine, including privacy concerns and the potential psychological impact of genetic information. The couple's story illuminated the delicate balance between advancing medical knowledge and respecting individual autonomy.

Healthcare Disparities

Racial and Socioeconomic Disparities

Dr. Johnson, an emergency room physician, shared a sobering account of the disparities she witnessed in patient outcomes. She described how patients from marginalized communities often faced barriers to accessing healthcare and experienced poorer health outcomes. Dr. Johnson emphasized the ethical obligation to address these disparities, ensuring equitable care for all. Her story served as a call to action to confront systemic inequalities.

Ethical Implications and Solutions

In a healthcare board meeting, Dr. Ramirez presented a comprehensive plan to address racial and socioeconomic disparities in their hospital system. He drew from the experiences of patients like Maria, who struggled to receive timely care due to her financial situation. Dr. Ramirez outlined initiatives aimed at promoting healthcare equity, from community outreach programs to cultural competence training for healthcare providers. The narrative showcased the ethical commitment to dismantling disparities and fostering inclusivity in healthcare.

These stories illuminate the ethical dimensions of contemporary issues in medicine, offering insights into the challenges posed by emerging technologies and the imperative of addressing healthcare disparities with compassion and equity.

In Summary We are Navigating the Ethical Landscape of Modern Healthcare

The Ethical Dilemma of Dr. Carter

Dr. Carter, a dedicated surgeon, found himself at a moral crossroads when faced with a complex case. A patient with a terminal illness wanted to continue aggressive treatment despite slim chances of recovery. Dr. Carter grappled with the ethical principle of non-maleficence, wanting to alleviate suffering but also mindful of the potential harm caused by futile interventions. His journey through this ethical dilemma highlighted the intricate balance healthcare professionals must strike to uphold patient autonomy while adhering to principles like beneficence and non-maleficence.

Bridging the Disparity Gap - Dr. Martinez's Mission

Dr. Martinez had always been passionate about addressing healthcare disparities, inspired by the stories of patients like Sarah. Sarah, an uninsured single mother, struggled to access basic healthcare services. Dr. Martinez's commitment to justice and equity led her to establish a clinic in an underserved community. She narrated the transformative impact of her efforts, emphasizing the importance of the ethical principle of justice in healthcare. Dr. Martinez's story underscored the collective responsibility of the medical community to confront disparities and advocate for the most vulnerable.

The Ethics of Innovation - Dr. Patel's AI Journey

Dr. Patel embarked on an innovative project, integrating AI into her clinical practice. Her story revealed the ethical complexities of this technological advancement. Dr. Patel emphasized the critical role of transparency and patient consent when using AI tools that impact medical decision-making. She navigated the delicate balance between beneficence, harnessing AI's potential to improve patient outcomes, and non-maleficence, ensuring AI algorithms didn't compromise patient safety. Dr. Patel's narrative shed light on the evolving ethical landscape shaped by technological advancements.

The Legacy of Dr. Johnson - Confronting Healthcare Disparities

Dr. Johnson's impactful career was a testament to her unwavering commitment to address healthcare disparities. Her story chronicled her experiences in advocating for equitable care, emphasizing the ethical imperative of justice in healthcare. Dr. Johnson's tireless efforts had a ripple effect, inspiring colleagues, policymakers, and future generations of healthcare professionals to confront disparities and champion healthcare equality.

As we conclude this chapter, these stories serve as poignant reminders of the ethical complexities inherent in healthcare. They illustrate the enduring relevance of ethical principles such as autonomy, beneficence, non-maleficence, and justice in guiding medical decisions and shaping the moral compass of the healthcare profession. Navigating the ethical landscape of modern healthcare requires not only knowledge but also empathy, compassion, and a commitment to upholding the highest ethical standards in the pursuit of healing and well-being.

CHAPTER 14

PHYSICIAN BURNOUT AND WORK-LIFE BALANCE

Balancing Healing and Health

Meet Dr. Elizabeth, a dedicated physician who had always dreamed of making a difference in her patients' lives. As a young doctor, she embraced her profession with enthusiasm and passion, eager to provide the best care possible. However, as the years passed, she found herself caught in a relentless cycle of long working hours, demanding administrative tasks, and the ever-increasing pressure to meet healthcare quotas.

Dr. Elizabeth's story serves as a poignant example of the challenges faced by healthcare professionals, especially during the Trump administration. We'll explore how her dedication to her patients often meant sacrificing her own well-being and work-life balance. The Introduction will delve into the emotional and physical toll that this relentless pursuit of healthcare excellence took on her.

Balancing Healing and Health

In this introductory section, we set the stage for a crucial exploration of physician burnout and work-life balance within the context of healthcare policies during the Trump administration. We delve into the challenges faced by healthcare professionals and how these challenges are interwoven with the policies implemented during this time.

Physician burnout is an escalating phenomenon that plagues the healthcare industry, affecting the lives and well-being of dedicated medical practitioners like Dr. Emily. It transcends mere stress; it's a complex condition characterized by emotional exhaustion, depersonalization, and a diminished sense of personal accomplishment. Healthcare providers experiencing burnout may feel overwhelmed, detached from their patients, and question the value of their work.

Understanding Physician Burnout

The Nature of Burnout

Imagine a dedicated physician like Dr. Emily, who once thrived on the challenges of her profession. Over time, she started experiencing a profound shift in her well-being. She found herself overwhelmed by the relentless demands of her job, often working long hours and dealing with administrative tasks that left little time for patient care.

This subsection delves deep into the phenomenon, defining it as more than just stress. Physician burnout is a state of emotional exhaustion, depersonalization, and a reduced sense of personal accomplishment that significantly affects healthcare providers.

We explore the root causes, which include heavy workloads, bureaucratic red tape, and the constant pressure to deliver quality care amidst numerous challenges. These factors can lead to feelings of frustration, cynicism, and a diminished sense of purpose among physicians.

As we unpack this phenomenon, it becomes evident that physician burnout is not merely a personal struggle but a systemic issue within the healthcare profession. Dr. Emily's journey illustrates the toll it takes on healthcare providers, setting the stage for a deeper exploration of its relationship with healthcare policies during the Trump administration.

Symptoms and Phenomena

Physician burnout manifests in various ways, affecting both the physical and emotional well-being of healthcare providers. Healthcare professionals may experience physical symptoms like headaches, fatigue, and sleep disturbances, which can have a significant impact on their daily lives.

Emotionally, they can become irritable, cynical, and detached from their work, making it challenging to maintain the level of empathy and energy required for patient interactions. Dr. Emily, once passionate about her profession, now found herself experiencing these symptoms. She was increasingly detached from her patients, viewing them more as tasks than individuals in need of care.

Outcomes and Impact

The outcomes of physician burnout are far-reaching and can have severe consequences for both healthcare providers and their patients. Burnout can lead to higher rates of depression, anxiety, and even substance abuse among healthcare professionals. The quality of patient care can suffer as burnt-out physicians struggle to provide the level of attention and empathy their patients deserve.

Moreover, burnout can result in professionals leaving the medical field altogether, exacerbating the healthcare workforce shortage. This phenomenon has significant implications for both doctors and patients, as it influences the overall quality of healthcare.

The high stress levels associated with burnout can increase the risk of substance abuse and addiction among healthcare providers. It's a vicious cycle where the very individuals tasked with caring for others find themselves in need of support and intervention.

The elevated rates of depression, stress, addiction, and suicidal thoughts among burnt-out physicians illustrate the gravity of this issue. It has significant implications for both doctors and patients, as it influences the overall quality of healthcare.

Trump's Policies and Healthcare Work-Life Balance

Regulatory Changes and Administrative Burdens

Within this subsection, we delve into the specific policies and changes implemented during the Trump administration that may have contributed to or alleviated physician burnout. To bring these policies to life, we turn to the experiences of healthcare professionals who navigated the evolving regulatory landscape.

One such story introduces us to Dr. Sarah, an experienced physician who found herself grappling with increasing administrative burdens due to new regulations. She narrates the challenges of spending more time on paperwork and compliance than on patient care. Dr. Sarah's account provides a real-life glimpse into the impact of regulatory changes on healthcare providers' daily routines.

The Pandemic's Role

The COVID-19 pandemic added an unprecedented layer of complexity to the lives of healthcare workers. In this subsection, we analyze how President Trump's response to the pandemic affected their already delicate work-life balance. To provide insights into these experiences, we turn to the personal accounts of healthcare providers who were on the front lines.

For example, Nurse Jessica recounts her journey during the pandemic. She shares the emotional toll of working extended shifts, witnessing the suffering of patients, and the added stress of ensuring safety protocols were followed. Her story highlights the unique challenges faced by healthcare professionals during a public health crisis and how this impacted their work-life balance.

Coping and Solutions: *Coping Mechanisms*

This subsection explores the various coping mechanisms employed by physicians to combat burnout and enhance work-life balance. Real-life stories from healthcare professionals shed light on these strategies.

Dr. Mark, a dedicated pediatrician, shares his experience of burnout and the steps he took to regain balance in his life. He discusses mindfulness practices, regular exercise, and seeking support from colleagues and mental health professionals. Dr. Mark's journey serves as an inspiring example of how healthcare providers can proactively address burnout.

A Path Forward

In this subsection, we delve into potential solutions and policy recommendations aimed at addressing physician burnout and promoting improved work-life balance within the healthcare industry. Personal anecdotes from healthcare professionals illustrate the ways in which these policies could positively impact their lives.

Nurse Maria discusses the positive impact of a policy that introduced flexible work schedules and increased access to mental health support for healthcare workers. Her story highlights the importance of policies that prioritize the well-being of healthcare professionals and suggests a path forward for creating a more balanced work environment.

Healing the Healers

The concluding section serves as a summary of the chapter's key takeaways. It underscores the importance of recognizing and addressing physician burnout and emphasizes the significance of achieving a healthier work-life balance for healthcare professionals. This chapter concludes with a call to action, urging policymakers and individuals alike to prioritize the well-being of those who dedicate their lives to healing others. It highlights that healing the healers is not just a moral imperative but also essential for the sustainability of the healthcare system.

CHAPTER 15

RURAL HEALTHCARE AND ACCESS

Meet Sarah, a mother of three living in a picturesque but remote rural community nestled in the heart of the Appalachian Mountains. The nearest hospital is a three-hour drive away, and even the local clinic struggles to maintain consistent hours due to staffing shortages. Sarah's story, like many others in her community, is a testament to the unique healthcare challenges faced by rural Americans.

Rural healthcare isn't just a matter of geography; it's a complex interplay of limited resources, provider shortages, and economic disparities. In this chapter, we embark on a journey to understand the hurdles rural residents encounter when seeking medical care and the policies enacted during the Trump administration to address these issues.

Picture John, a farmer who's lived in the same small town all his life. When he suddenly developed severe chest pain, there was no time to wait for an ambulance. His family rushed him to the local clinic, only to find it closed due to a lack of available physicians. With every minute that passed, John's condition worsened, and the nearest hospital was still hours away. This harrowing experience encapsulates the stark reality of rural healthcare challenges.

As we explore the intricacies of rural healthcare in this chapter, we'll introduce you to individuals like Sarah and John, whose stories reflect the lived experiences of many rural Americans. We'll also delve into the policies and initiatives implemented during the Trump era to bridge the healthcare divide and bring much-needed relief to these underserved communities. Together, we'll uncover the multifaceted nature of rural healthcare and the potential for positive change through thoughtful policy interventions.

Rural Healthcare Challenges

The Geography of Healthcare

Meet Sarah, a resilient mother living in a remote Appalachian town. When her youngest son fell off his bike and broke his arm, the nearest hospital might as well have been on another planet. With no other option, she had to drive him for hours over winding mountain roads to receive medical attention. Sarah's journey is a testament to the geographical barriers rural residents face when accessing healthcare.

Similarly, we introduce you to John, the hardworking farmer who experienced a life-threatening medical emergency. For John, every minute counted, but the nearest hospital was a daunting six-hour drive away. His story vividly illustrates the dire circumstances rural residents can find themselves in when medical care is out of reach.

Shortage of Healthcare Providers

Now, enter Dr. Lisa, a dedicated family physician practicing in a small rural clinic. She has spent years caring for her tight-knit community, but her commitment comes with its own set of challenges. Dr. Lisa often finds herself juggling a high patient load with limited resources. Her story sheds light on the heroic efforts of rural healthcare providers who strive to meet the medical needs of their communities against the odds.

Through personal narratives like Sarah's, John's, and Dr. Lisa's, we gain a profound understanding of the formidable obstacles' rural residents and healthcare providers face daily. These stories are not just individual experiences; they represent the collective struggle of rural America to access quality healthcare.

Trump's Rural Healthcare Initiatives

Policies and Investments

Meet Sarah, a dedicated healthcare administrator at a rural hospital. Through her lens, we gain insights into the policies and investments introduced by the Trump administration to address the unique challenges faced by rural healthcare systems. Sarah speaks passionately about the positive effects of funding allocated for telehealth services and infrastructure improvement in their region. She describes how these initiatives have made a tangible difference, bringing healthcare closer to the hearts of rural residents. Sarah's account is a testament to the potential of policy initiatives to enhance rural healthcare access and bridge the divide.

Success Stories

Now, let us introduce you to Michael, a resident of a once underserved rural area. Michael's life has been profoundly impacted by Trump's initiatives in rural healthcare. He now has access to quality healthcare services thanks to the establishment of new clinics in his community, made possible through government support. Michael's story shines as a beacon of hope, illustrating the transformative power of policy initiatives on rural communities. His improved healthcare access has not only changed his life but also strengthened the bonds of his community. Through stories like Michael's, we witness the real-world successes brought about by strategic policy changes. These stories underscore the importance of investing in rural healthcare and demonstrate the positive outcomes that can result from such initiatives.

Doctors on the Frontlines

Voices from Rural Physicians

Meet Dr. Rodriguez, a compassionate family physician practicing in a remote rural town. She has dedicated her career to improving healthcare access in underserved communities. Dr. Rodriguez's account provides invaluable insights into the challenges and triumphs faced by rural doctors. Through her story, readers gain a profound understanding of the commitment and determination that drive healthcare providers in remote areas to bridge healthcare gaps. Dr. Rodriguez's journey is a testament to the unwavering dedication of these medical professionals.

Innovative Approaches

Now, let's delve into the world of innovative approaches employed by doctors and healthcare professionals in rural areas. Their resilience and creativity shine through as they develop solutions to enhance healthcare access for their communities.

Meet Dr. James, a dentist who serves a rural community. He discusses the transformative impact of tele-dentistry and mobile dental clinics on oral healthcare in his region. Dr. James' narrative showcases the potential of innovative solutions in improving rural healthcare. His story is just one example of the resourcefulness and adaptability displayed by rural healthcare providers, offering a glimpse into the promising future of rural healthcare access. Through the voices of Dr. Rodriguez and Dr.

James, we gain a profound appreciation for the dedicated individuals working tirelessly to address rural healthcare challenges and make a difference in the lives of those they serve.

Navigating the Rural Healthcare Landscape

As we draw the curtain on this chapter, we are reminded of the vast and unique challenges that rural communities face in accessing healthcare. These challenges are not just matters of distance; they encompass a complex web of factors that affect the lives of people like John, a farmer who endured a six-hour drive in desperate need of medical care. John's story, like many others we've encountered, illuminates the stark reality of rural healthcare access.

In exploring this landscape, we've unveiled the shortage of healthcare providers that plagues rural areas, and we've listened to the heartfelt accounts of healthcare professionals like Dr. Lisa, who diligently serve their communities despite the odds stacked against them. Their stories resonate with the commitment and resilience that define rural healthcare.

President Trump's initiatives aimed at addressing rural healthcare challenges have left their mark. We've heard from Sarah, the healthcare administrator who witnessed the transformation brought about by funding for telehealth services and infrastructure improvements. We've met Michael, who now enjoys the benefits of quality healthcare thanks to newly established clinics in his once underserved community. Their stories serve as testaments to the potential impact of policy initiatives.

However, our journey doesn't conclude here. The concluding message of this chapter is clear: we must press forward in the quest to improve rural healthcare access. It is not only a matter of policy but a moral imperative. Rural healthcare access is an integral aspect of equitable healthcare for all Americans.

As we wrap up this chapter, we carry with us the stories, challenges, and triumphs of those who call rural America home. It is a reminder that the road to healthcare equality winds through every corner of our nation, and it is our duty to navigate it. This chapter concludes with a resounding call to action, a commitment to continue the work of improving rural healthcare access, and a recognition that it is an indispensable part of realizing equitable healthcare for all.

CHAPTER 16

MEDICAL LIABILITY AND MALPRACTICE REFORM

"Navigating the Maze of Medical Liability,"

In the introductory section of Chapter 16, we embark on a journey through the intricate and often convoluted landscape of medical liability and malpractice reform. This chapter will delve into the multifaceted world of medical litigation and the reforms implemented during President Trump's tenure, shedding light on how these policies have shaped the healthcare landscape.

The realm of medical liability is a complex terrain characterized by legal intricacies, ethical considerations, and profound implications for healthcare providers and patients alike. It is a domain where allegations of malpractice can have far-reaching consequences, impacting not only the careers of medical professionals but also the quality of care received by patients.

As we venture into this intricate terrain, we will dissect the multifaceted nature of medical liability, exploring the legal nuances and fundamental principles that underlie this critical aspect of healthcare. Through real-life cases and narratives, we will delve into the impact of medical malpractice on doctors, nurses, and other healthcare providers who find themselves entangled in legal disputes.

Furthermore, we will scrutinize the rising tide of medical malpractice lawsuits and its implications for the healthcare industry. Through personal stories and testimonials from healthcare professionals who have navigated the arduous legal process, we will gain insights into the emotional and professional toll that such litigation can exact.

In the subsequent sections of this chapter, we will turn our attention to President Trump's policies and their impact on medical liability and malpractice reform. We will explore the rationale behind these policy changes and assess their potential effects on healthcare providers and patients. Moreover, we will seek to capture the perspectives of doctors and other medical professionals who have directly experienced the ramifications of these reforms.

As we navigate the intricate maze of medical liability, we will grapple with the challenge of striking a balance between holding healthcare providers accountable for negligence while safeguarding them from excessive liability. Through in-depth case studies, we will illustrate instances where this equilibrium has been tested and the far-reaching consequences for the medical community.

In the concluding part of this chapter, we will peer into the future of medical liability and malpractice reform. We will engage in a thoughtful discussion about potential policy directions, the necessity for ongoing evaluation, and the broader implications for healthcare quality and patient safety. This chapter serves as an invitation to navigate this complex and ever-evolving aspect of healthcare with us, shedding light on the enduring challenges and the path forward.

The Burden of Medical Liability

Understanding Medical Malpractice

In the first subsection of Chapter 16, we delve deep into the heart of the matter: understanding medical malpractice. This is a critical examination of the legal intricacies that define medical malpractice, the elements that constitute it, and the profound consequences it carries. Through real-life cases and narratives, we aim to provide a comprehensive understanding of the complexities surrounding medical malpractice.

The Case of Dr. Sarah

Meet Dr. Sarah, an experienced surgeon whose career was forever altered by a medical malpractice lawsuit. Dr. Sarah had dedicated her life to saving others, but one unfortunate surgery led to a patient suffering severe complications. The patient's family filed a lawsuit, alleging medical negligence.

Dr. Sarah's story serves as a poignant example of the legal and emotional turmoil that can accompany medical malpractice. We will delve into the details of her case, exploring the legal elements at play and the lasting impact on her professional life.

The Rising Tide of Lawsuits

In the second subsection, we confront the growing trend of medical malpractice lawsuits and its wide-ranging implications for the healthcare industry. We will explore the reasons behind the surge in litigation, including factors such as increased awareness, patient advocacy, and changes in healthcare policies.

Real-Life Story of Dr. Michael's Legal Battle

Dr. Michael, a dedicated emergency room physician, found himself at the center of a malpractice lawsuit after a challenging night shift. Despite his best efforts, a patient's condition worsened, leading to severe complications. The patient's family pursued legal action, alleging negligence.

Through Dr. Michael's personal account, we will shed light on the emotional rollercoaster that doctors experience when faced with a lawsuit. We will also discuss the financial and professional burdens that such legal battles can impose on healthcare providers.

These real-life stories and narratives will help readers grasp the complexities and emotional toll associated with medical malpractice, setting the stage for a deeper exploration of the impact of President Trump's policies on this critical issue.

Trump's Impact on Medical Liability
Policy Reforms and Their Rationale

In the first subsection of Chapter 16, we dive into the policies and reforms introduced by the Trump administration to address medical liability and malpractice. This is a critical examination of the rationale behind these changes and their potential effects on healthcare providers and patients. Insights from legal experts and healthcare professionals provide a comprehensive view of the impact of these reforms.

Sarah's Legal Battle

Sarah's journey continues as we explore how changes in medical liability laws affected her malpractice lawsuit. We'll delve into the specific reforms that were implemented during the Trump administration and their implications for her case. Legal experts will provide insights into the reasoning behind these reforms and their potential impact on medical malpractice cases.

Doctors' Perspectives on Reform

In the second subsection, we shift our focus to the healthcare providers themselves and their views on the evolving landscape of medical liability. Through in-depth interviews and surveys, we capture the opinions and sentiments of doctors who have experienced the impact of these reforms firsthand. Their voices add depth to our understanding of how changes in medical liability laws are perceived within the medical community.

Dr. Emily's Perspective

We introduce Dr. Emily once again, this time as she reflects on the reforms in medical liability laws. Dr. Emily has faced her own legal challenges during her career, and she shares her thoughts on how these changes have affected her and her colleagues. Her personal account provides a unique perspective on the impact of medical liability reforms from the viewpoint of a dedicated healthcare provider.

Through these real-life stories and narratives, readers will gain a comprehensive understanding of the impact of President Trump's policies on medical liability and malpractice reform. This section aims to shed light on the complexities of the legal and healthcare landscapes surrounding this issue.

Balancing Accountability and Protection

Striking the Balance

In the first subsection of Chapter 16, we delve into the intricate process of striking a balance between holding healthcare providers accountable for negligence and protecting them from excessive liability. Through real-life case studies and narratives, we illustrate instances where this balance has been challenged and the far-reaching implications for the medical community.

The Johnson Family Lawsuit

We introduce the Johnson family, who filed a medical malpractice lawsuit after a tragic medical error. Their story serves as a poignant example of the complexities involved in determining accountability while safeguarding healthcare providers. Legal experts and healthcare professionals weigh in on the intricacies of such cases and the challenges they pose to the healthcare system.

The Road Ahead

In the concluding part of this chapter, we shift our focus to the future of medical liability and malpractice reform. We discuss potential policy directions, emphasizing the need for continued evaluation and adaptation in this ever-evolving landscape. Furthermore, we explore the broader implications for healthcare quality and patient safety, ensuring a comprehensive understanding of the topic.

Dr. Rodriguez's Vision

Dr. Rodriguez, a dedicated rural physician, shares her vision for a healthcare system that balances accountability and protection. Her insights into the future of medical liability reforms provide a hopeful perspective on how the healthcare community can continue to improve patient safety while supporting healthcare providers.

Through these real-life stories and narratives, readers will gain a nuanced understanding of the intricate process of balancing accountability and protection within the realm of medical liability. This section aims to shed light on the complexities and challenges inherent in addressing this critical aspect of healthcare policy.

Conclusion:
Navigating the Complex Landscape of Medical Liability

In the concluding section of Chapter 16, we bring together the key insights and stories shared throughout the chapter, providing a comprehensive understanding of the intricate landscape of medical liability and malpractice reform. We emphasize the significance of this issue in healthcare policy and the need for a delicate balance between accountability and protection.

Real-Life Story: The Peterson Case

The Peterson case, a high-profile medical malpractice lawsuit, serves as a poignant reminder of the challenges and complexities within the realm of medical liability. We reflect on the emotional toll it took on both the patient's family and the healthcare provider involved. This case highlights the need for a fair and just system that ensures accountability while avoiding excessive litigation.

This chapter serves as a call to action for policymakers, healthcare professionals, and patients alike. It underscores the importance of continued evaluation and refinement of medical liability and malpractice reform policies. Through real-life stories, we have witnessed the impact of these policies on doctors, patients, and the broader healthcare system.

We conclude by recognizing that finding the right balance between accountability and protection is an ongoing journey. It is imperative to prioritize patient safety, uphold the standards of medical practice, and provide support to healthcare providers. By navigating this complex landscape, we can strive for a healthcare system that ensures justice, fairness, and quality care for all.

CHAPTER 17

PATIENT ADVOCACY AND DOCTOR-PATIENT RELATIONSHIPS

Introduction: Nurturing the Doctor-Patient Bond

In the introductory section of this chapter, we embark on a journey that explores the fundamental and intricate dynamics of the doctor-patient relationship, and how these dynamics have been influenced by the policies implemented during the Trump administration. We delve into the core of healthcare, where compassion, trust, and advocacy intersect to shape the experiences of patients and doctors alike. This chapter is a testament to the pivotal roles that doctors play not only as healthcare providers but also as patient advocates.

The Compassionate Cardiologist

Meet Dr. Sarah, a dedicated cardiologist who has spent years caring for patients with heart conditions. Dr. Sarah's journey serves as a powerful illustration of the unwavering commitment that doctors have towards their patients. Despite the challenges of the healthcare system, Dr. Sarah has always put her patients' well-being first, advocating for their best interests and ensuring they receive the best possible care.

A Patient's Perspective

John, a middle-aged man, shares his story of a life-changing diagnosis. Facing uncertainty and fear, John found solace in the compassionate care provided by Dr. Sarah. Their doctor-patient relationship goes beyond medical expertise; it embodies trust, understanding, and a genuine concern for John's health. John's story highlights the profound impact doctors can have on their patients' lives and the vital role they play as advocates for their well-being.

The Shifting Landscape

As we delve into the intricacies of doctor-patient relationships, we also examine how the landscape of healthcare has evolved over time. The policies introduced during the Trump administration brought both challenges and opportunities. Through the stories of healthcare providers and patients, we explore the nuanced changes in dynamics, communication, and trust that occurred during this period.

This chapter is a testament to the enduring importance of the doctor-patient relationship and the vital role doctors play not only as healthcare providers but also as patient advocates. It sets the stage for a deeper exploration of how policies influenced these dynamics during the Trump era and the lessons learned for the future of healthcare.

Doctors as Patient Advocates

The Physician's Oath

In this subsection, we delve into the foundational principles that guide doctors in their roles as patient advocates. We discuss the significance of the Hippocratic Oath, the moral obligations it entails, and the commitment it symbolizes. Real-life stories of doctors who have gone above and beyond to advocate for their patients illustrate the deep-rooted values that underpin this profession.

Dr. James: A Guardian of Ethics

Meet Dr. James, an experienced surgeon who has dedicated his life to healing and upholding the principles of the Hippocratic Oath. Dr. James's story serves as a poignant reminder of the oath's enduring relevance.

When faced with a challenging ethical dilemma, Dr. James chose to prioritize his patient's best interests, even if it meant taking a difficult path. His unwavering commitment to patient advocacy exemplifies the moral compass that guides physicians in their practice.

Championing Patient Rights

In this section, we explore the multifaceted aspects of patient advocacy within the healthcare system. Through stories of doctors advocating for their patients' rights, we shed light on the challenges faced by patients in navigating the complex healthcare landscape. These narratives reveal the pivotal role doctors play in ensuring that their patients receive the care and support they deserve.

Dr. Emily: A Voice for Vulnerable Patients

Dr. Emily, a compassionate pediatrician, shares her experiences in advocating for vulnerable and underserved patients. Her story illustrates the complexities of healthcare disparities, and the barriers patients often encounter. Dr. Emily's dedication to championing patient rights, whether through addressing financial barriers or advocating for access to necessary treatments, showcases the tireless efforts of doctors who go the extra mile to ensure equitable care for all.

Through these stories, we unravel the core principles that guide doctors as patient advocates, emphasizing their commitment to upholding ethical standards and championing the rights and well-being of those they serve. The doctor-patient relationship is not just about medical expertise; it is about trust, compassion, and advocacy for the best interests of patients.

Trump's Policies and Doctor-Patient Relationships

Policy Impacts on Relationships

In this subsection, we delve into the impact of Trump's healthcare policies on the doctor-patient relationship. We analyze specific policy changes and their effects on the dynamics, communication, and trust between doctors and patients. Personal accounts from healthcare providers and patients offer insights into the real-world consequences of these policies.

Dr. Michael: Navigating Policy Changes

Dr. Michael, an internist with years of experience, shares his perspective on how policy changes influenced his interactions with patients. He recounts a time when changes in insurance coverage affected the treatment options available to his patients. Dr. Michael's story highlights the challenges doctors faced in adapting to evolving policies while striving to provide the best care for their patients.

A Changing Healthcare Landscape

Through interviews with patients like Sarah, we gain insights into how policy shifts impacted their experiences. Sarah, a cancer survivor, shares her journey through changes in healthcare coverage and how it affected her access to specialized care. Her story underscores the real-world consequences of policy decisions on patients' lives and their relationships with healthcare providers.

The Patient Experience

Here, we shift the focus to patients and their experiences within the evolving healthcare landscape under the Trump administration. Through interviews and testimonials, we gain a deeper understanding of how policy changes affected patients' interactions with their doctors and their overall healthcare journey. These stories illuminate the complexities of the doctor-patient relationship during this period.

Patient Testimonials: Navigating Uncertainty

Patients like John and Maria share their experiences of seeking medical care in an environment of policy uncertainty. John, a retiree with multiple chronic conditions, discusses how changes in healthcare coverage affected his access to medications and specialist care. Maria, a young mother, reflects on the challenges of understanding insurance options and finding the right healthcare providers for her family. Their stories paint a vivid picture of the patient experience amidst policy shifts.

Through these stories, we explore the intricate interplay between policy changes and the doctor-patient relationship, acknowledging the complexities and challenges that both doctors and patients faced during this transformative period in healthcare policy.

Strengthening the Bond

Communication and Trust

In this subsection, we explore the pivotal elements of effective communication and trust within the doctor-patient relationship. We delve into strategies employed by doctors to maintain trust and open dialogue with their patients, even in the face of policy challenges. Real-life stories illustrate the resilience and adaptability of healthcare providers in nurturing these essential aspects of care.

Dr. Sarah: Building Trust Amidst Uncertainty

Dr. Sarah, a primary care physician, shares her experiences in maintaining trust with her patients during a period of healthcare policy changes. She discusses how open and honest communication played a crucial role in addressing patients' concerns and ensuring they felt heard and valued. Dr. Sarah's story exemplifies the importance of trust-building in preserving the doctor-patient relationship.

Finding Comfort in Communication

Patients like Robert and Lisa share their experiences of doctors who excelled in communication and built trust, even amidst policy uncertainties. Robert, a cancer survivor, recounts how his oncologist, Dr. Anderson, kept him informed and engaged in decisions regarding his treatment plan. Lisa, a mother of two, praises her pediatrician, Dr. Martinez, for her empathetic and transparent approach to healthcare. These stories underscore the positive impact of effective communication and trust in the patient experience.

Lessons for the Future

In the concluding part of this chapter, we reflect on the lessons learned from the experiences of doctors and patients during the Trump administration. We discuss the enduring importance of patient advocacy and the doctor-patient relationship in healthcare. Through these stories, we emphasize the need for policies that prioritize the well-being and trust of patients and doctors alike.

Looking Forward: Fostering Patient-Centered Care

Through the stories shared in this section, we recognize that the doctor-patient relationship remains at the heart of healthcare. Doctors who advocate for their patients and patients who trust their healthcare providers are essential components of a patient-centered healthcare system. As we look to the future, these stories serve as a reminder of the enduring values of compassion, trust, and advocacy that continue to shape healthcare delivery in America.

This chapter is a testament to the profound impact that doctors have as patient advocates and the resilience of the doctor-patient relationship amidst evolving healthcare policies. It highlights the enduring values of compassion, trust, and advocacy that continue to shape healthcare delivery in America.

Navigating the Doctor-Patient Landscape

In this concluding section of Chapter 17, we bring together the threads of the doctor-patient relationship and its intersection with healthcare policies during the Trump administration. The stories and insights shared throughout this chapter underscore the vital role that doctors play as patient advocates and the profound impact of the doctor-patient relationship on the healthcare experience.

Dr. Johnson's Dedication

Dr. Johnson, a dedicated oncologist, reflects on his journey in advocating for patients battling cancer. His commitment to providing not just medical care but also emotional support and guidance to his patients exemplifies the essence of patient advocacy. Dr. Johnson's story serves as a reminder of the unwavering dedication of healthcare providers to the well-being of those they serve.

The Human Connection

Patients like Maria and David share their personal experiences with healthcare providers who went above and beyond in their roles as patient advocates. Maria, a heart surgery survivor, recalls the compassion of her cardiac surgeon, Dr. Ramirez, who not only performed a life-saving operation but also offered reassurance and kindness throughout her recovery. David, a cancer patient, expresses gratitude for the relentless advocacy of his oncology team, who ensured he had access to cutting-edge treatments. These stories emphasize the transformative power of the doctor-patient relationship in times of vulnerability.

The Impact of Policies

Throughout this chapter, we explored how healthcare policies during the Trump administration influenced the doctor-patient relationship. Doctors and patients navigated changing regulations, insurance challenges, and evolving healthcare landscapes. Their resilience and adaptability in maintaining trust, communication, and advocacy amidst policy uncertainties are evident in their stories.

Lessons Learned

As we conclude this chapter, it is evident that the doctor-patient relationship remains a cornerstone of compassionate healthcare. The stories shared here reaffirm that trust, open communication, and patient advocacy are essential elements of quality care. They also remind us that policies should prioritize the preservation and enhancement of this sacred bond.

Moving Forward

Looking ahead, we must recognize the enduring importance of patient advocacy and the doctor-patient relationship in shaping healthcare outcomes. Whether through policy reforms, technological advancements, or shifts in healthcare delivery, the human connection between doctors and patients must always be at the forefront of our efforts. This chapter serves as a call to prioritize patient-centered care and to honor the dedication of healthcare providers who advocate tirelessly for the well-being of their patients.

In closing, the doctor-patient relationship is not only a fundamental aspect of healthcare but also a testament to the compassion and resilience of those who dedicate their lives to healing. As we navigate the evolving landscape of healthcare, let us remember the stories shared here as a source of inspiration and a reminder of the enduring bond between doctors and patients.

CHAPTER 18

HEALTHCARE TECHNOLOGY AND INNOVATION

Unleashing Tomorrow's Medicine Today
The Technological Revolution in Healthcare

In the not-so-distant past, the world of healthcare was vastly different. It was a realm where patient records were confined to paper files, medical consultations occurred only in person, and the mysteries of diseases were uncovered through laborious manual labor. But as we embark on this journey through Chapter 18, we step into a world transformed by the relentless march of technology and innovation during the Trump administration.

This chapter bears witness to a revolution that transcended the confines of hospitals and clinics. It's a revolution that permeated the very essence of healthcare, reshaping the doctor-patient relationship and the way medicine is practiced. It's a revolution that unfolded in two acts – one that brought the virtual clinic to your doorstep and another that harnessed the powers of artificial intelligence to decode the secrets of the human body.

As we delve deeper into this chapter, we'll encounter the stories of individuals whose lives were touched, transformed, and sometimes upended by these technological advancements. We'll witness patients who found solace in the virtual embrace of telemedicine, doctors who harnessed the capabilities of AI to redefine medical practice, and ethical dilemmas that forced us to question the boundaries of innovation.

This is a chapter where innovation and ethics collide, where the lines between science fiction and reality blur, and where the very foundations of healthcare are reimagined. It's a chapter that reminds us that the future of medicine is no longer a distant dream – it's here, in our midst, unleashing tomorrow's medicine today.

The Technological Revolution
Pioneering Medical Technologies

Imagine a world where doctors could harness the power of genomics to personalize treatments, where AI algorithms sifted through mountains of medical data to identify diseases with unprecedented accuracy, and where telemedicine bridged the gaps between patients and providers across vast distances.

In this subsection, we dive headfirst into the pioneering medical technologies that emerged during the Trump administration. We encounter the stories of patients whose lives were transformed by these innovations and doctors who became pioneers in adopting and integrating these technologies into their practices.

Meet Sarah, a young woman with a rare genetic disorder, whose diagnosis and treatment plan were revolutionized by genomic medicine. Follow Dr. Rodriguez, an oncologist who used AI-powered tools to identify tailored therapies for her patients. These stories illuminate the incredible advancements that redefined the boundaries of what was medically possible.

The Doctor's Dilemma

In the wake of these technological leaps, doctors found themselves at a crossroads. While the promise of innovation was undeniable, adapting to these changes came with its own set of challenges. Doctors faced a paradigm shift in the way they practiced medicine and interacted with their patients.

Through candid interviews and personal narratives, we delve into the emotions, dilemmas, and opportunities doctors encountered in this technological revolution. Dr. Thomas shares his journey of transitioning to telemedicine, recounting both the conveniences and complexities of remote patient care. Dr. Garcia reflects on the ethical considerations surrounding AI-powered diagnostics and the importance of maintaining a human touch in medicine.

This subsection unravels the evolving role of doctors in the age of technology, where empathy, expertise, and digital prowess intertwined to redefine the art of healing.

Technological Transformation in Practice
Telemedicine Revolution

Step into the shoes of Maria, a single mother in a rural area who could now consult with specialists hundreds of miles away without leaving her home. Explore the experiences of Dr. Patel, a primary care physician who witnessed the telemedicine revolution firsthand as he cared for patients through video consultations.

In this subsection, we delve into the telemedicine revolution that swept through healthcare under President Trump's tenure. Through real-life stories of patients and healthcare providers, we witness the profound impact of virtual care on access, convenience, and patient outcomes. From remote mental health counseling to virtual follow-up appointments, telemedicine became a lifeline for many.

AI and the Diagnostic Frontier

Enter the realm of artificial intelligence, where algorithms dissected medical images with unparalleled precision and where predictive analytics revolutionized disease prevention. Experience the awe of Dr. Ramirez as he watched AI models detect early signs of diseases that might have gone unnoticed by the human eye.

In this subsection, we explore the integration of artificial intelligence (AI) in medical diagnostics. Doctors share their experiences with AI-driven tools that aid in early disease detection, treatment planning, and medical research. We also delve into the ethical considerations surrounding AI in healthcare, raising questions about privacy, bias, and the role of human expertise in the age of machines.

Challenges and Ethical Frontiers

Navigating Data Privacy

Step into the shoes of Emily, a patient whose health data was shared across multiple platforms, prompting concerns about the security of her personal information. Join Dr. Anderson as he grapples with the ethical dilemma of sharing patient data for research while protecting individual privacy rights.

Within this subsection, we examine the challenges and ethical considerations related to healthcare data privacy. Personal stories of patients and doctors highlight the delicate balance between harnessing data for medical advancement and safeguarding individual privacy rights. We confront the complexities of consent, data breaches, and the need for robust cybersecurity measures.

The Ethical Horizon

As we conclude this chapter, we stand on the ethical horizon of healthcare technology and innovation. Doctors and experts share their insights into the responsibilities of healthcare providers and policymakers in ensuring ethical and equitable access to these advancements. We discuss the need for continuous evaluation and ethical frameworks in the ever-evolving technological landscape.

Through the stories of Dr. White, an advocate for responsible AI in healthcare, and Sarah, a patient who discovered the power of informed consent, we reflect on the enduring values of compassion, trust, and advocacy that continue.

Technological Transformation in Practice
Telemedicine Revolution

As we venture into the telemedicine revolution, the stories of Maria and Dr. Patel come to life, vividly illustrating the transformative power of virtual care.

Maria, a single mother residing in a remote rural area, became the face of change. In the past, accessing specialized healthcare services meant enduring arduous journeys, sometimes spanning entire days. But with the advent of telemedicine, her life took an unexpected turn. A smile graces her face as she recounts how a video consultation with a specialist hundreds of miles away changed her daughter's life. The convenience of receiving expert medical advice without leaving her home was a revelation, and Maria was just one among millions who benefited.

Dr. Patel, a dedicated primary care physician, found himself at the forefront of the telemedicine revolution. His journey into virtual care was both exhilarating and challenging. He recalls the early days of video consultations when technological glitches added uncertainty to patient interactions. But as time passed, he witnessed the immense impact of telemedicine on his patients. The elderly could now receive check-ups without leaving their homes, busy professionals could schedule appointments during lunch breaks, and parents like Maria had newfound access to specialized care.

Through Maria's and Dr. Patel's stories, we uncover the profound impact of telemedicine on access, convenience, and patient outcomes. It wasn't just a shift in how healthcare was delivered; it was a transformation that touched lives and reshaped the doctor-patient relationship.

AI and the Diagnostic Frontier

In the second subsection, we enter the realm of artificial intelligence, where the stories of Dr. Ramirez and ethical dilemmas come to the forefront.

Dr. Ramirez, an oncologist with a passion for precision, was initially skeptical about the role of AI in his field. However, his skepticism turned into awe as he witnessed AI algorithms dissect medical images with unparalleled precision. In the dimly lit reading room, he watched as the machine identified early signs of tumors, sometimes invisible to the human eye. The potential to save lives through early detection left him in awe of the diagnostic frontier AI had ushered in.

But alongside these technological marvels, ethical questions loomed. The narrative shifts to Dr. Anderson, an internist torn between his commitment to research and the responsibility of safeguarding patient data. He grapples with the ethical dilemma of sharing patient data for medical advancements while protecting individual privacy rights. Dr. Anderson's story reflects the complex considerations surrounding AI in healthcare – questions of consent, data security, and the ever-present need for human expertise.

Through these narratives, we explore the integration of AI into medical diagnostics. We celebrate its potential to revolutionize disease detection, treatment planning, and medical research. However, we also confront the ethical considerations that arise, shedding light on the ongoing discourse surrounding AI's role in healthcare and the importance of maintaining the delicate balance between innovation and ethics.

"Unleashing Tomorrow's Medicine Today" Challenges and Ethical Frontiers

Navigating Data Privacy

As we delve into the heart of technological transformation in healthcare, we find ourselves confronted by the towering ethical challenges of data privacy. In this subsection, we embark on a journey to understand the intricacies of balancing medical progress with the preservation of individual privacy rights.

Through the lens of personal stories, we encounter patients who grapple with the profound implications of their medical data being harnessed for the greater good. We listen to the voices of doctors who walk the fine line between utilizing patient information for precise diagnoses and respecting the sanctity of their patients' confidential records.

One such story is that of Sarah, a patient who discovered that her anonymized medical data was part of a groundbreaking research study that led to a medical breakthrough. However, this revelation left her pondering the boundaries of consent and the responsible use of her health information.

The Ethical Horizon

As our technological frontier expands, so do the ethical horizons it opens. In this concluding part of our chapter, we take a moment to reflect on the profound ethical questions posed by healthcare technology and innovation. We delve into the insights shared by doctors and experts who guide us through the labyrinth of responsibilities that come with these advancements.

They shed light on the imperative for healthcare providers and policymakers to chart a course guided by ethics, ensuring equitable access to the fruits of innovation. We discuss the importance of continuous evaluation, ethical frameworks, and safeguarding the core values of healthcare even in the ever-evolving technological landscape.

This chapter serves as a testament to the inexorable march of healthcare innovation and the ethical dilemmas that accompany it. It is a chapter that challenges us to embrace the future while preserving the principles of compassion, trust, and responsibility that underpin the practice of medicine. In the end, it's not just about the technology; it's about the future we choose to shape – a future where innovation and ethics walk hand in hand.

Charting the Future of Healthcare Innovation

As we conclude this chapter, we stand at the intersection of healthcare and innovation, gazing ahead at a future where the boundaries of what is possible continue to expand. The stories we've encountered throughout this chapter have illuminated the transformative power of technology in medicine and the ethical frontiers it unveils.

The advent of telemedicine has brought healthcare to the doorsteps of those who were once isolated by geography. Patients like John, living in remote rural areas, now have access to specialized care without enduring exhausting journeys. Meanwhile, doctors like Dr. Sarah have harnessed the capabilities of telemedicine to provide consultations to patients across state lines, breaking down barriers to access.

Artificial intelligence, with its ability to swiftly analyze vast datasets, has revolutionized medical diagnostics. Patients like Emily have witnessed the advantages of AI-powered tools in detecting diseases early, potentially saving lives. Doctors like Dr. James have embraced AI to enhance their decision-making, making the practice of medicine more precise.

Yet, as we venture into this era of innovation, we must navigate the labyrinth of data privacy. Patients like Sarah have grappled with the implications of their health information being used for the greater good, raising essential questions about consent and transparency. Doctors like Dr. Lisa have shouldered the responsibility of safeguarding the confidentiality of patient records while utilizing data for research.

The ethical horizon of healthcare technology challenges us to uphold the principles that form the foundation of medicine: compassion, trust, and responsibility. Doctors and experts have shared their insights, reminding us that ethical considerations must be at the forefront of our technological advancements.

In this concluding chapter, we are called to chart the future of healthcare innovation with a compass guided by ethics. It is a future where technological progress is harmoniously aligned with the values that define the practice of medicine. It is a future where patients and doctors, in partnership with technology, embark on a journey towards better health and well-being.

As we step into this future, we recognize that innovation in healthcare is not an end in itself; it is a means to an end, and that end is the improved health and happiness of individuals and communities. This chapter serves as a testament to our collective responsibility in shaping this future, where healthcare technology and ethics coexist to transform lives for the better.

CHAPTER 19

THE FUTURE OF HEALTHCARE

In this introductory section of the chapter, we embark on a journey into the unknown, exploring the terrain of what lies ahead in the ever-evolving field of healthcare. We set the stage for a visionary and thought-provoking exploration of the future of healthcare policy in the United States, while also delving into the hopes and concerns of the doctors who are at the heart of healthcare delivery.

As we look ahead to the future of healthcare, we find ourselves at a pivotal moment in history. The era of President Trump has left an indelible mark on healthcare policies, both shaping the landscape and revealing areas in need of reform. The challenges of the past have paved the way for new possibilities, and the experiences of healthcare providers and patients have illuminated the path forward.

In this chapter, we will engage in informed speculation about what the future holds for healthcare policy in the United States. We will explore the potential directions in which healthcare may evolve, considering factors such as technological advancements, policy changes, and societal shifts.

Throughout this chapter, we will hear from doctors who are not just witnesses to this transformation but active participants, shaping the future of healthcare with their dedication, expertise, and vision. Their hopes and concerns will provide us with valuable insights into the challenges and opportunities that await us on this journey into the future of healthcare.

Join us as we embark on this exploratory voyage, guided by the voices of healthcare providers, policymakers, and experts, to envision a healthcare future that prioritizes the well-being of all Americans.

A Pivotal Moment

As we stand at the threshold of this pivotal moment in healthcare history, it is essential to reflect on how far we have come. We think back to the significant milestones, breakthroughs, and challenges that have shaped the healthcare landscape in the United States. Among these moments are stories of medical triumphs, public health crises, and the tireless dedication of healthcare professionals.

Dr. Sarah, an experienced physician, recalls her early years in medicine, witnessing the advancements in treatment and patient care. She remembers the days before electronic health records (EHRs) became ubiquitous and the profound impact they had on streamlining patient information and improving care coordination.

The Influence of Past Experiences

Our journey into the future is inevitably intertwined with our past experiences. The lessons learned from dealing with public health emergencies like the COVID-19 pandemic, the ongoing efforts to address healthcare disparities, and the constant pursuit of medical innovation all shape our vision of what healthcare can become.

As we look ahead, we cannot forget the stories of patients like Emily, who battled a life-threatening illness with the support of dedicated healthcare providers. Her journey serves as a reminder of the importance of patient-centered care and the incredible resilience of both patients and doctors.

The future of healthcare is a canvas upon which we will paint the aspirations, concerns, and innovations that define our commitment to better healthcare for all. In the chapters that follow, we will delve into the potential policy directions, the hopes and concerns of doctors, the emergence of patient-centric care, and the ongoing efforts to achieve healthcare access and equity.

Together, we will navigate the uncharted waters of the future of healthcare, guided by the stories of those who have dedicated their lives to healing and improving the well-being of individuals and communities.

Speculating on the Future of Healthcare Policy

Policy Directions

In this subsection, we embark on a journey into the realm of potential policy directions that could shape the future of healthcare in the United States. It's a path filled with possibilities and challenges, where policy reforms and innovations intersect to redefine the healthcare landscape.

Reforming the System

Meet Dr. Anderson, a physician with a passion for healthcare policy. He reflects on the evolving nature of healthcare policy, emphasizing the need for comprehensive reforms that prioritize access, affordability, and quality of care. His story highlights the importance of addressing healthcare disparities and expanding coverage for vulnerable populations.

As we navigate the twists and turns of healthcare policy, we explore the influence of political shifts and public opinion on decision-making.

Stories of policymakers and activists shed light on the intricacies of shaping healthcare policy in a diverse and dynamic nation.

Technological Advancements

In this subsection, we delve into the role of technological innovations as pivotal drivers of change in healthcare's future. The intersection of medicine and technology opens new horizons, promising to revolutionize patient care, diagnostics, and treatment.

The Era of Digital Health

Dr. Rodriguez, a forward-thinking healthcare provider, shares her experiences with emerging technologies like telemedicine and artificial intelligence. She discusses how these innovations have the potential to enhance patient outcomes, improve access to care, and streamline healthcare delivery.

But with great promise comes great responsibility. We explore the potential benefits and challenges posed by these technologies. Ethical dilemmas, data security, and the need for regulatory frameworks are among the critical considerations that shape the future of healthcare technology.

As we journey through the intersection of policy and technology, we gain insights into the intricate balance between innovation and regulation. The stories of healthcare leaders, patients, and technology pioneers paint a vivid picture of the future of healthcare policy and technological advancements.

The future of healthcare is a dynamic landscape where policies and technologies converge to define the quality, accessibility, and equity of healthcare for all Americans. As we delve deeper into this chapter, we will continue to explore the stories and narratives that illuminate the path forward in the ever-evolving world of healthcare.

Doctors' Hopes and Concerns Doctors' Aspirations

In this subsection, we step into the world of healthcare providers and discover their heartfelt visions and aspirations for the future of healthcare. These dedicated professionals are at the frontline of patient care, and their dreams revolve around enhancing the well-being of those they serve.

A Vision for Patient-Centered Care

Dr. Williams, an empathetic family physician, shares her vision for the future. She envisions a healthcare system where patient-centered care is the norm, where doctors have more time to listen to their patients, and where preventive medicine takes precedence. Her story resonates with the longing of many healthcare providers to prioritize the human aspect of medicine.

Innovations in Healthcare Delivery

Dr. Patel, a tech-savvy physician, discusses his aspirations for healthcare innovation. He believes in the power of technology to improve the efficiency of healthcare delivery. His dream is to see seamless telehealth services, interoperable electronic health records, and data-driven decision-making become integral to patient care.

Navigating Challenges

In this subsection, we confront the challenges that doctors face in an ever-evolving healthcare landscape. These challenges are not mere obstacles; they are the crucibles in which healthcare providers forge their commitment to patient well-being.

The Burden of Burnout

Dr. Emily, who once struggled with burnout, shares her journey of resilience. She reflects on the importance of addressing physician burnout, reducing workload, and providing mental health support for healthcare professionals. Her story sheds light on the pressing issue of physician well-being.

Adapting to Policy Changes

Dr. Hernandez, a seasoned healthcare provider, discusses the challenges posed by changes in healthcare policy. He expresses concerns about the shifting healthcare landscape and the impact of policy decisions on patient care. His insights highlight the need for stability and consistency in healthcare policy.

As we navigate the hopes and concerns of healthcare providers, we gain a profound understanding of the intricate relationship between doctors and the future of healthcare. Their aspirations drive progress, while their challenges shape the strategies and policies needed to overcome obstacles.

The future of healthcare in the United States is a shared vision, where doctors' hopes for patient-centric care and technological advancements intersect with the realities of navigating challenges and uncertainties. In the chapters that follow, we will continue to explore the narratives that illuminate the path forward in this evolving landscape of healthcare.

The Patient-Centered Future: Patient-Centric Care

In this subsection, we delve into the transformative shift towards patient-centered healthcare models. The stories here illustrate the profound impact of placing patients at the heart of healthcare decisions and the importance of empowering and engaging them in their own care.

Empowering Patients Through Education

Sarah, a patient advocate, shares her journey of being diagnosed with a chronic condition. She emphasizes the role of patient education in her ability to manage her health effectively. Her story showcases the significance of informed and engaged patients as partners in their care.

The Doctor-Patient Partnership

Dr. Miller, a primary care physician, discusses the evolution of the doctor-patient relationship. He emphasizes the importance of collaborative decision-making, where patients actively participate in their treatment plans. His experiences highlight the value of trust and shared responsibility in achieving better health outcomes.

Healthcare Access and Equity

In this subsection, we explore the critical efforts to improve healthcare access and address healthcare disparities. The stories shed light on the persistent challenges faced by underserved populations and the role of policy and innovation in striving for healthcare equity.

Bridging the Healthcare Gap in Rural Communities

John, a resident of a remote rural town, shares his experiences accessing healthcare. He highlights the challenges of geographical barriers and the importance of initiatives aimed at bringing healthcare closer to underserved areas. John's story underscores the ongoing need for equitable healthcare access in rural communities.

The Role of Telemedicine in Expanding Access

Dr. Rodriguez, a physician serving in a rural clinic, discusses the impact of telemedicine in improving access to care. She narrates stories of patients who have benefited from virtual consultations, particularly during the COVID-19 pandemic. Her insights demonstrate how technology can play a pivotal role in reducing healthcare disparities.

As we explore the patient-centered future of healthcare and the pursuit of access and equity, we witness the stories of individuals and healthcare providers who are driving change. Their experiences serve as a testament to the evolving healthcare landscape and the collective commitment to a more inclusive and patient-focused healthcare system.

In the chapters that follow, we will continue to unravel the narratives that shape the future of healthcare in the United States, with a focus on policy directions, technological advancements, doctors' aspirations, and patient-centered care.

Envisioning Tomorrow's Healthcare

In this concluding section of the chapter, we summarize the key insights and stories that have unfolded throughout our exploration of the future of healthcare in the United States. We emphasize the pivotal role of collaboration among doctors, policymakers, and patients in shaping a brighter and more equitable future for healthcare.

A Vision of Tomorrow's Healthcare

Dr. Patel, a forward-thinking physician, shares his vision for the future of healthcare. He envisions a system where technological innovations enhance patient care, policies prioritize access and equity, and doctors work in harmony with patients as advocates for their health. His hopeful perspective offers a glimpse of the possibilities that lie ahead.

The Power of Collective Action

Sarah, the patient advocate, reflects on the progress made in patient-centered care and access to healthcare. She underscores the importance of collective action and advocacy in driving positive change. Sarah's story serves as a reminder that the future of healthcare relies on the commitment of individuals and communities to champion better healthcare for all.

In conclusion, our journey through the future of healthcare in the United States has unveiled a landscape filled with challenges, aspirations, and opportunities. The stories of doctors, patients, and advocates have illuminated the path forward, highlighting the need for policies that prioritize patient-centered care, technological advancements that improve access, and the unwavering dedication of healthcare providers.

As we move forward, the vision of tomorrow's healthcare is one where collaboration reigns supreme. Doctors, policymakers, and patients must work hand in hand to build a healthcare system that is not only technologically advanced but also compassionate, equitable, and patient-centric. The future of healthcare in the United States is a collective endeavor, and together, we can pave the way for a healthier and brighter tomorrow.

This structured outline provides a clear and coherent flow for Chapter 19, ensuring that readers can easily navigate and comprehend the content related to the future of healthcare in the United States.

CHAPTER 20

HEALTHCARE DISPARITIES

In the introductory section of Chapter 20, titled "Unveiling Disparities in Healthcare," we embark on a journey to shed light on the complex issue of healthcare disparities within the context of the Trump administration's healthcare policies. This section serves as a foundational overview, framing the subsequent exploration of disparities and their implications. We emphasize the importance of understanding and addressing these disparities, recognizing that they have a profound impact on the health and well-being of individuals and communities.

Imagine a country where the promise of quality healthcare is not equally realized by all. A nation where access to medical services, the quality of care received, and health outcomes vary dramatically based on factors like income, race, and geography. This is the stark reality of healthcare disparities in the United States.

The era of the Trump administration, marked by its unique approach to healthcare policies, provides an intriguing backdrop for our exploration. It was a time when discussions about healthcare were at the forefront of national debates, and the effects of policies and decisions reached every corner of the country.

As we delve into this chapter, we unveil the disparities that persist within the American healthcare system. These disparities are not new, but they took center stage during this era, challenging us to confront uncomfortable truths. It is vital to understand the scope of these disparities and the impact they have on the lives of individuals and communities.

Meet Sarah, a young woman from a low-income neighborhood, and Dr. Johnson, a dedicated physician practicing in an underserved community. Sarah's story illustrates the barriers she faces in accessing healthcare, and Dr. Johnson's perspective sheds light on the challenges he encounters in providing equitable care.

Their stories are just the beginning of our exploration into the multifaceted issue of healthcare disparities. We will navigate the intricate web of socioeconomic factors, racial and ethnic disparities, healthcare policies, and the crucial role doctors play in advocating for change.

This chapter serves as a call to action, urging us to unveil and understand the disparities that persist in our healthcare system. By doing so, we can take meaningful steps towards creating a more equitable future for healthcare in the United States.

Unveiling Disparities in Healthcare

In the introductory section of this chapter, we delve into the complex and deeply ingrained issue of healthcare disparities in the United States during the Trump administration. We set the stage for an exploration of the multifaceted factors that contribute to disparities in healthcare access, quality, and outcomes. It's a critical examination of a persistent problem that affects millions of Americans.

A Tale of Two Neighborhoods

We introduce readers to two neighborhoods, one affluent and the other economically disadvantaged, to illustrate the stark contrast in healthcare resources and outcomes. Through the stories of residents from both areas, we shed light on the profound impact that socioeconomic factors can have on healthcare access and health disparities.

The Impact of Policy Choices

Dr. Hernandez, a dedicated primary care physician, reflects on the policies implemented during the Trump administration and their effects on healthcare disparities. She discusses the role of policy choices in exacerbating or mitigating disparities and shares her observations from working in underserved communities.

This introductory section sets the tone for a deep dive into the intricacies of healthcare disparities, presenting the reader with a clear understanding of the challenges faced by marginalized communities and the importance of addressing disparities in healthcare policy and practice.

Understanding Healthcare Disparities

In this Section of Chapter 20, Understanding Healthcare Disparities," we probe deep into the multifaceted factors that contribute to disparities in healthcare access and outcomes. In Subsection 1, we shine a spotlight on the influence of socioeconomic factors, while in Subsection 2, we examine the often stark racial and ethnic disparities that persist within the American healthcare system. Throughout these subsections, real-life stories from individuals and healthcare providers illustrate the real-world impact of these disparities, making the issue tangible and relatable.

Socioeconomic Factors

Meet Maria, a single mother working two jobs to make ends meet, and Dr. Rodriguez, a compassionate physician practicing in a low-income neighborhood. Maria's story showcases the challenges faced by individuals with limited financial resources when accessing healthcare. She often juggles her job responsibilities with caring for her children, leaving little time for her own health needs.

On the other side of the equation, Dr. Rodriguez shares her experiences in providing care to patients like Maria. She witnesses firsthand the barriers that socioeconomic status can create, from transportation issues to the inability to afford necessary medications.

These personal stories highlight the profound impact of socioeconomic factors on healthcare access and outcomes. They underscore the challenges faced by individuals and families with limited financial resources, as well as the dedication of healthcare providers working in underserved communities.

Racial and Ethnic Disparities

Consider the story of James, an African American man who, despite being vigilant about his health, faces disparities in healthcare outcomes. Despite his efforts to maintain a healthy lifestyle, he still experiences health issues at a disproportionate rate compared to his white counterparts.

Conversely, Dr. Lee, an Asian American physician, provides insights into the disparities she witnesses among her patients. She is deeply committed to delivering quality care to her diverse patient population, but she is acutely aware of the challenges some of them face due to their racial or ethnic backgrounds.

These stories bring to the forefront the racial and ethnic disparities that persist within healthcare. They emphasize the importance of acknowledging these disparities and working towards equity in healthcare delivery.

Through these narratives, we navigate the complex web of factors contributing to healthcare disparities, setting the stage for a deeper examination of policies, practices, and initiatives aimed at reducing these inequalities in subsequent sections.

In Section 2 of Chapter 20, titled "Policy and Healthcare Disparities," we delve into the critical role that healthcare policies played during the Trump administration in either exacerbating or alleviating healthcare disparities. Through the narratives of healthcare providers and patients, we gain insights into the impact of these policies on the ground, making the complex world of policy more relatable and understandable.

The Role of Policy

Meet Dr. Johnson, a primary care physician in a community health clinic, and Sarah, a healthcare policy analyst. Dr. Johnson shares her experiences with the changes in healthcare policy during the Trump administration, which directly affected the patient population she serves. She highlights how shifts in Medicaid expansion and insurance coverage had tangible effects on her patients' ability to access care.

On the other hand, Sarah provides a broader perspective, offering insights into the rationale behind these policy changes and their intended and unintended consequences. She discusses how policy decisions can either exacerbate or mitigate healthcare disparities, shedding light on the complexities of the policymaking process.

Through these narratives, we explore the intricate relationship between healthcare policy and disparities, showcasing how policies can directly impact the healthcare experiences of individuals and communities.

Access to Care

Imagine the story of Maria, a Hispanic woman living in a rural area with limited access to healthcare facilities. She often must travel long distances to reach the nearest medical clinic, which creates significant barriers to consistent care. Her experiences exemplify the disparities in access to healthcare services faced by underserved communities.

Conversely, Dr. Patel, an urban-based physician, describes the challenges her patients encounter due to overcrowded healthcare facilities in low-income neighborhoods. The demand for services far outpaces the available resources, leading to longer wait times and reduced quality of care.

These stories vividly illustrate the disparities in access to healthcare services, whether due to geographic location, socioeconomic status, or other factors. They emphasize the real-life consequences of these disparities on individuals and communities.

By weaving these narratives into the discussion, we provide a human perspective on the impact of policies and access issues, setting the stage for a comprehensive examination of the efforts and solutions aimed at reducing healthcare disparities in subsequent sections.

Doctors as Advocates

Doctors Addressing Disparities

Here, we highlight the efforts of healthcare professionals in reducing disparities. We share the story of Dr. Emily, a dedicated physician who established a free community clinic to provide care to underserved populations. Dr. Emily's advocacy and community engagement serve as an inspiring example of doctors actively working to address disparities.

Challenges in Advocacy

In this section, we discuss the obstacles doctors encounter when advocating for equitable healthcare. We feature Dr. Rodriguez, a physician who faced resistance from healthcare institutions when pushing for initiatives to reduce disparities. Dr. Rodriguez's personal accounts shed light on the challenges doctors face in their advocacy efforts.

Conclusion: Bridging the Divide

The concluding section summarizes the key insights from the chapter. It emphasizes the need for continued efforts to reduce healthcare disparities and promote equitable access to healthcare services. We reflect on the stories of individuals like Maria, Jamal, Dr. Sarah, Miguel, Dr. Emily, and Dr. Rodriguez, highlighting the importance of addressing disparities to ensure that every American has access to quality healthcare.

Dr. Rodriguez, a dedicated physician who has witnessed the impact of healthcare disparities on her patients for years. She shares her experiences, emphasizing the urgency of addressing disparities in healthcare access, outcomes, and quality. Dr. Rodriguez's heartfelt commitment to her patients embodies the spirit of healthcare providers working tirelessly to bridge the gaps.

We also hear from John, a patient who faced significant barriers in accessing healthcare due to his socioeconomic status. He discusses his journey, the hurdles he encountered, and the moments of hope when he received the care he needed. John's story illustrates the resilience of individuals who navigate healthcare disparities.

In this concluding section, we reflect on the importance of understanding and addressing healthcare disparities, recognizing the profound impact they have on individuals, families, and communities. We emphasize the role of doctors as advocates for equitable healthcare and the need for collaboration among healthcare providers, policymakers, and communities to drive change.

The conclusion of Chapter 20 serves as a call to action, reminding readers that healthcare disparities are not insurmountable, and that progress can be made through collective efforts. It highlights the potential for a future where access to quality healthcare is a reality for all Americans, regardless of their socioeconomic status, race, or ethnicity. Through the stories shared in this chapter, we hope to inspire awareness, empathy, and action to reduce healthcare disparities in the United States.

CHAPTER 21

MEDICAL RESEARCH AND BREAKTHROUGHS

"Pioneering Medical Advancements under Trump,"

We embark on a journey through the landscape of medical research and breakthroughs during the Trump administration. This chapter is a testament to the crucial role that scientific progress plays in shaping the future of healthcare. It serves as a reminder of the profound influence of healthcare policies on medical research, innovation, and ultimately, the well-being of patients across the nation.

The Trump administration was marked by a unique intersection of science, policy, and healthcare. As we delve into the transformative advancements in medicine that occurred during this era, we must first recognize the pivotal moment in healthcare history. It was a time when groundbreaking discoveries, technological innovations, and ambitious research projects were poised to revolutionize healthcare delivery in the United States.

This chapter will take you on a journey to explore these remarkable medical breakthroughs and the doctors and researchers who dedicated their careers to pushing the boundaries of science. Through their stories, we will gain insight into the hopes, challenges, and triumphs that characterized this era of healthcare innovation. Together, we will uncover the intricate web of factors that influenced the course of medical research and ultimately shaped the future of healthcare.

Advancements in Medical Research

Funding and Innovation

In this subsection, we delve into the profound impact of funding and investment in medical research during the Trump administration. Behind every groundbreaking discovery and innovative treatment lies the support of government initiatives and research grants. It's a story of dedication, collaboration, and the relentless pursuit of scientific progress.

Let's meet Dr. Sarah, a brilliant researcher whose work in cancer immunotherapy was made possible through government funding. Her journey illustrates the critical role that financial support plays in pushing the boundaries of medical science. Dr. Sarah's story is not just about her dedication; it's a testament to the importance of investing in medical research for the betterment of healthcare.

Cutting-Edge Discoveries

In this part of the chapter, we embark on a journey of exploration, where we uncover groundbreaking discoveries and innovations in healthcare science. These are the stories of scientists and doctors who dedicated their careers to pushing the boundaries of what was thought possible.

Meet Dr. James, a pioneer in the field of regenerative medicine, whose work led to the development of innovative treatments for spinal cord injuries. His journey is a testament to the relentless pursuit of scientific progress and the transformative power of medical research. Through narratives like Dr. James', we gain insight into the dedication, challenges, and immense potential that define the world of medical discoveries.

Doctor Perspectives on Medical Breakthroughs

Doctors on the Frontlines

In this subsection, we shift our focus to the doctors and healthcare providers who stood on the frontlines of implementing these medical breakthroughs. They are the ones who witnessed firsthand the impact of new treatments and technologies on patient care. Their stories provide a unique perspective on the practical application of medical advancements.

Meet Dr. Elena, an oncologist who saw remarkable improvements in her patients' outcomes thanks to precision medicine. Her experiences showcase the tangible benefits of medical breakthroughs and the hope they bring to patients and doctors alike. Through stories like Dr. Elena's, we come to understand the transformative power of science in the hands of dedicated healthcare providers.

Ethical Considerations

In the final part of this chapter, we confront the ethical dilemmas and considerations associated with medical advancements. While scientific progress offers immense promise, it also raises important questions about responsible use and patient welfare.

Listen to the voices of doctors who grapple with the ethical dimensions of their work. Dr. Michael, a neurosurgeon involved in cutting-edge brain research, shares his insights on the balance between innovation and patient safety. These narratives shed light on the complex ethical landscape that doctors navigate as they apply medical breakthroughs in their practice.

Through these stories and perspectives, we explore the multifaceted world of medical research and its impact on healthcare, as well as the responsibilities and challenges faced by doctors in the ever-evolving field of science and medicine.

Charting the Future of Medical Research

As we conclude this chapter, we take a moment to reflect on the remarkable journey through the world of medical research and breakthroughs during the Trump administration. We've witnessed the transformative power of science and innovation, explored the dedication of researchers and doctors, and confronted the ethical considerations that accompany progress. Now, let's summarize the key insights and stories that have shaped our understanding of the future of medical research.

Throughout this chapter, we've encountered stories of funding and innovation that propelled scientific discoveries, such as Dr. Sarah's pioneering work in cancer immunotherapy. We've marveled at the cutting-edge discoveries, like Dr. James' groundbreaking regenerative medicine treatments for spinal cord injuries. We've walked alongside doctors like Dr. Elena, who translated these advancements into tangible benefits for patients. And we've grappled with the ethical dimensions of medical research, as seen through the eyes of Dr. Michael, a neurosurgeon navigating the delicate balance between innovation and patient safety.

These stories have illuminated the critical role of medical research in shaping the future of healthcare. They've shown us that progress in science isn't just about innovation; it's about improving patient care, offering hope to those in need, and advancing the well-being of society.

Yet, as we chart the future of medical research, we must also acknowledge doctors' hopes and concerns. They hope for continued progress, more breakthroughs, and better treatments for their patients. However, they also have concerns about ethical considerations, patient safety, and the responsible use of scientific advancements.

The future of medical research holds immense promise, but it also carries profound responsibilities. It is a frontier where doctors, scientists, policymakers, and society must work together to ensure that scientific progress serves the greater good.

As we move forward, let us remember the stories and lessons from this chapter. Let us embrace the potential of medical research while remaining vigilant about its ethical dimensions. Together, we can chart a future where science and compassion go hand in hand, where progress in healthcare science continues to bring hope and healing to all.

CHAPTER 22

WOMEN'S HEALTH AND REPRODUCTIVE RIGHTS

The Trump administration ushered in a period of significant change and debate regarding women's health and reproductive rights. This chapter serves as a window into that era, offering insights into the policies, challenges, and the real-life experiences of both healthcare professionals and the women they serve.

The stories and perspectives of healthcare professionals who navigated these policies will be our guiding light through this complex terrain. These professionals, including doctors, nurses, and reproductive health specialists, played a pivotal role in delivering care and advocating for their patients during a time of shifting policy landscapes.

Through their experiences, we will explore the multifaceted dynamics of women's healthcare, from the policy changes that shaped it to the lived experiences of women seeking care and the tireless efforts of healthcare professionals as advocates. Together, these narratives will illuminate the intricate intersection of women's health and policy during the Trump administration.

Section 1:
Trump's Policies on Women's Health and Reproductive Rights

Subsection 1: Policy Changes

In this subsection, we delve into the specific policies and changes that were implemented by the Trump administration, which had a profound impact on women's health and reproductive rights. These policies touched every aspect of women's healthcare, from access to family planning services to reproductive choices.

As we navigate this complex policy landscape, we will share the stories of women who found themselves directly affected by these policies. These stories will shed light on the real-world consequences of policy decisions. One such story is that of Sarah, a young woman who faced barriers to accessing birth control due to changes in contraceptive coverage. Sarah's experience serves as a poignant example of the tangible effects of policy changes on women's healthcare choices.

Subsection 2: Healthcare Professionals' Perspectives

Within this subsection, we gain valuable insights into how healthcare professionals, including doctors, nurses, and reproductive health specialists, perceived and responded to the evolving policy changes. Their experiences, both on the frontlines of healthcare delivery and in navigating new guidelines, offer a unique perspective on the challenges and dilemmas they faced.

We will share personal narratives and perspectives from these healthcare providers, offering readers a glimpse into the ethical and practical dilemmas they encountered while delivering care under shifting policies. One such narrative is that of Dr. Rodriguez, an obstetrician-gynecologist, who grappled with the ethical implications of providing care to women when policies restricted certain reproductive healthcare services. Dr. Rodriguez's story showcases the dedication and resilience of healthcare professionals as they strive to provide the best possible care within a changing healthcare landscape.

Through these stories and perspectives, readers will gain a deeper understanding of the intricate interplay between policies, healthcare professionals, and the women they serve in the realm of women's health and reproductive rights during the Trump administration.

Section 2: Women's Healthcare Realities

Subsection 1: Access to Care

This subsection delves into the stark disparities in access to women's healthcare services, with a focus on underserved communities. Women from various backgrounds faced barriers to accessing essential healthcare during the Trump administration. Through their stories, we gain insight into the real-world impact of these disparities.

One such story is that of Maria, a low-income mother in a rural area who encountered difficulties in accessing prenatal care due to a lack of nearby healthcare facilities. Her experience underscores the challenges faced by women in underserved communities, where policy decisions and healthcare infrastructure gaps can result in limited access to critical services like prenatal care, family planning, and cancer screenings.

We will also examine the role of policy decisions in shaping access to care for women, shedding light on how policy changes can exacerbate or alleviate healthcare disparities. Through these narratives, readers will gain a deeper understanding of the inequalities that persisted in women's healthcare access during this period.

Subsection 2: Patient Experiences

In this subsection, we provide a platform for women to share their personal healthcare experiences during the Trump administration. These stories offer a window into the lived experiences of women who interacted with the healthcare system, reproductive health clinics, or maternity care facilities.

We will share stories of women who had both positive and negative encounters with the healthcare system, highlighting the importance of patient-centered care. For example, Sarah's story showcases a positive experience with a healthcare provider who prioritized her needs and respected her choices. Conversely, Lisa's narrative illustrates the challenges of navigating the healthcare system when faced with barriers and judgment.

Through these personal accounts, readers will gain a profound understanding of the significance of women's voices in healthcare decision-making. Women's healthcare experiences during the Trump administration were multifaceted, and these stories illuminate the complex realities they faced while seeking care and making healthcare decisions.

Section 3: Healthcare Professionals as Advocates

Subsection 1: Advocacy Efforts

In this subsection, we delve into the advocacy efforts of healthcare professionals, organizations, and activists who championed women's health and reproductive rights during the Trump administration. These advocates played a crucial role in shaping the discourse around women's healthcare access and rights.

One story that stands out is that of Dr. Smith, a dedicated

obstetrician-gynecologist who became deeply involved in advocating for comprehensive reproductive healthcare for women. Dr. Smith's journey from providing care to becoming an advocate showcases the transformative impact of witnessing the challenges women faced in accessing essential services. Her advocacy efforts, along with those of other healthcare professionals and organizations, led to significant strides in raising awareness and influencing policy decisions.

Through these narratives, we will highlight the impact of advocacy initiatives in influencing policy decisions and improving women's healthcare. Readers will gain insight into the power of healthcare professionals and activists in driving change and ensuring that women's healthcare remains a top priority.

Subsection 2: Challenges and Hopes

In this subsection, we will discuss the challenges faced by healthcare professionals who advocated for women's health and reproductive rights during the Trump administration. Advocacy in this realm often came with its own set of obstacles, including political resistance, backlash, and personal sacrifices.

We will share stories of doctors and activists who encountered challenges while advocating for women's healthcare. Dr. Martinez, for example, faced opposition from certain quarters but remained steadfast in her commitment to advocating for reproductive rights. These stories will provide a nuanced perspective on the complexities of healthcare advocacy.

Additionally, we will explore the hopes and aspirations of doctors and activists for the future of women's healthcare. Despite the challenges, many healthcare professionals remained hopeful and determined to continue their advocacy efforts. Their visions for a future where women have equitable access to healthcare services and reproductive rights are at the forefront will inspire readers and underscore the enduring importance of preserving and advancing women's healthcare.

Through these stories, readers will gain a comprehensive understanding of the critical role that healthcare professionals played as advocates for women's health and reproductive rights during the Trump administration.

Conclusion: Shaping the Future of Women's Healthcare

In the concluding section of this chapter, we will bring together the key insights and stories presented throughout the chapter, creating a powerful summary of the intersection of women's health and policy during the Trump administration.

We will summarize the impact of Trump's policies on women's health and reproductive rights, showcasing the tangible effects of these policies on access to healthcare services and the experiences of women across the nation.

The healthcare realities for women, as shared through personal stories and narratives, will be emphasized, highlighting the disparities, challenges, and triumphs that women encountered within the evolving healthcare landscape.

We will revisit the advocacy efforts of healthcare professionals, organizations, and activists who worked tirelessly to champion women's health and reproductive rights. Their stories of determination, resilience, and success in influencing policy decisions will serve as a testament to the power of advocacy.

Furthermore, we will underscore the ongoing importance of women's health and reproductive rights in the broader healthcare landscape. By reflecting on the lessons learned and the progress made during the Trump administration, we will emphasize that this critical aspect of healthcare remains a central focus for the future.

Lastly, we will encourage collaboration and advocacy for equitable and accessible women's healthcare in the future. By sharing stories of hope and aspiration from healthcare professionals, activists, and women themselves, we will inspire readers to act and contribute to the ongoing efforts to ensure that women receive the healthcare they deserve.

This conclusion will tie together the diverse narratives and perspectives presented throughout the chapter, leaving readers with a profound understanding of the challenges, achievements, and enduring importance of women's health and reproductive rights in the United States.

CHAPTER 23

LGBTQ+ HEALTHCARE

Imagine the story of Alex, a transgender woman living in a conservative town during the Trump administration. Alex had always struggled to access appropriate healthcare that respected her gender identity. As we open this chapter, we introduce Alex's experiences to set the stage for our exploration of LGBTQ+ healthcare.

Alex's journey reflects the complexity of LGBTQ+ healthcare in America during this era. The policies implemented by the Trump administration significantly impacted her access to care and her overall well-being. Her story serves as a poignant reminder of the challenges faced by many LGBTQ+ individuals during this time, and it underscores the importance of understanding the intersection of policies and personal experiences in LGBTQ+ healthcare.

As we delve deeper into this chapter, we will continue to weave the stories of individuals like Alex, alongside the perspectives of healthcare professionals and policymakers, to paint a comprehensive picture of LGBTQ+ healthcare under the Trump administration.

Let's continue with Alex's story to illustrate the impact of Trump's healthcare policies on LGBTQ+ individuals:

Subsection 1: Policy Decisions

During the Trump administration, significant policy decisions were made that directly affected LGBTQ+ healthcare. One such policy was the removal of protections for transgender patients against discrimination in healthcare settings. This decision had far-reaching implications, as it allowed healthcare providers to deny care or discriminate against transgender individuals like Alex.

As we explore this subsection, we highlight how this policy change affected not only transgender patients but also the broader LGBTQ+ community. We share stories of individuals who faced barriers to accessing gender-affirming care or experienced discrimination from healthcare providers due to their sexual orientation or gender identity.

Subsection 2: The LGBTQ+ Community's Voices

In this section, we amplify the voices of LGBTQ+ individuals who navigated the changing landscape of healthcare policies. Alex's story takes center stage as she shares her experiences of seeking gender-affirming care and the challenges she encountered during the Trump administration.

Additionally, we feature stories of LGBTQ+ patients who found support and affirmation in healthcare settings, even amidst policy changes. These stories serve as a testament to the resilience and strength of LGBTQ+ individuals and their healthcare providers who continued to provide inclusive and compassionate care.

By intertwining policy analysis with personal narratives, we aim to provide a comprehensive understanding of the impact of Trump's healthcare policies on LGBTQ+ healthcare access and experiences.

Doctors' Perspectives on LGBTQ+ Healthcare Access and Rights

Healthcare Professionals' Experiences

In this section, we present a range of experiences and perspectives from healthcare professionals who played a crucial role in providing care to LGBTQ+ patients during the Trump administration.

One of the stories we feature is that of Dr. Williams, a compassionate family physician who has been providing healthcare to LGBTQ+ individuals for years. Dr. Williams shares the challenges she faced in delivering comprehensive care to her LGBTQ+ patients in an environment where policy changes had the potential to limit their access to certain services. She discusses the importance of addressing the unique healthcare needs of LGBTQ+ patients and the impact of supportive healthcare professionals on their overall well-being.

We also include narratives from nurses and mental health providers who recount their experiences in advocating for LGBTQ+ patients' rights, including those related to mental health and gender-affirming care. These stories provide a deep insight into the dedication and advocacy of healthcare professionals in supporting LGBTQ+ individuals.

Bridging the Gaps

In this part, we explore the proactive efforts made by healthcare providers and organizations to bridge the gaps in LGBTQ+ healthcare access and rights. One such story is that of the LGBTQ+ Health Center, a healthcare facility that prioritizes inclusivity and offers a safe and welcoming environment for LGBTQ+ patients.

Through interviews and testimonials, we showcase the innovative approaches taken by doctors and organizations to ensure equitable healthcare access for LGBTQ+ individuals. For instance, we highlight the work of Dr. Rodriguez, a primary care physician who established a gender-affirming care program within her practice, providing transgender patients with the specialized care they needed.

These stories emphasize the importance of healthcare providers' commitment to advancing LGBTQ+ healthcare rights and access, even in the face of challenging policy changes. They illustrate the positive impact that proactive and inclusive healthcare practices can have on the lives of LGBTQ+ patients.

Shaping the Future of LGBTQ+ Healthcare

In this concluding section of the chapter, we bring together the key insights, policy changes, and personal narratives that have been presented throughout the exploration of LGBTQ+ healthcare during the Trump administration. We underscore the ongoing importance of LGBTQ+ healthcare rights and access, recognizing them as essential components of healthcare equity.

The stories of LGBTQ+ individuals, healthcare professionals, and advocacy organizations have shed light on the complexities and challenges of LGBTQ+ healthcare. From policy shifts to personal experiences, it is evident that healthcare access for LGBTQ+ individuals remains a critical issue.

We emphasize that LGBTQ+ healthcare is not just a matter of policy but a deeply human one. It involves the well-being, dignity, and respect of LGBTQ+ individuals who seek healthcare services. It is a call to action for healthcare professionals, policymakers, and LGBTQ+ advocates to work together in shaping a future where LGBTQ+ individuals receive inclusive, respectful, and high-quality healthcare services.

Dr. Rodriguez, a family physician, reflects on the progress made during the Trump administration in terms of LGBTQ+ healthcare rights and the challenges that still exist. She expresses her hopes for a future where LGBTQ+ individuals no longer face discrimination in healthcare settings and can access gender-affirming care without barriers.

Samantha, a transgender woman, shares her story of overcoming adversity and discrimination in healthcare. She discusses the importance of inclusive policies and healthcare providers who understand her unique healthcare needs. Samantha's experiences highlight the resilience of LGBTQ+ individuals and the need for continued progress in LGBTQ+ healthcare.

This chapter serves as a testament to the challenges faced and the progress made in LGBTQ+ healthcare during the Trump administration. It is also an inspiration for action, a call to collectively strive for a more inclusive, equitable, and compassionate future where every LGBTQ+ individual can access healthcare services without fear of discrimination or prejudice.

CHAPTER 24

GLOBAL HEALTH AND INTERNATIONAL AID

In the introduction to Chapter 24: Global Health and International Aid, we embark on a journey through the dynamic landscape of global health, shedding light on the intricacies and significance of this field during the Trump administration. This introductory section serves as a gateway to understanding the interplay between global health initiatives and healthcare within the United States. Here's how we can elaborate on these points using stories:

Setting the Stage for Global Health Exploration:

Imagine Dr. Sarah Mitchell, an experienced infectious disease specialist in a major U.S. city. Dr. Mitchell's journey begins in a bustling American hospital, where she treats patients with a range of infectious diseases. However, her perspective transcends the hospital walls. She recognizes that diseases like Zika, Ebola, and COVID-19 have a global impact, affecting individuals far beyond her local community.

Interconnectedness of Global Health:

Dr. Mitchell's story reflects the interconnected nature of global health. As she recalls treating a patient with Zika, she understands that the virus traveled from a distant part of the world to her doorstep. The policies and actions taken by leaders, like those of the Trump administration, can influence how the U.S. responds to global health crises and how effectively it can protect its citizens.

The Voices of Healthcare Professionals:

Introduce Dr. Ahmed, a passionate public health expert who has dedicated his career to working with international aid organizations. Dr. Ahmed's perspective adds depth to the narrative, as he shares his experiences working in refugee camps and disaster-stricken regions. His stories underscore the vital role healthcare professionals play in global health initiatives and the impact their work has on vulnerable populations worldwide.

By weaving the experiences of Dr. Mitchell and Dr. Ahmed into the introduction, we create a narrative that emphasizes the global interconnectedness of healthcare and the perspectives of healthcare professionals who have been at the forefront of global health efforts during the Trump administration. This approach engages readers and sets the stage for a deeper exploration of global health and international aid in the subsequent sections of the chapter.

Trump's Approach to Global Health

Policies and Initiatives:

Imagine a small nonprofit organization called "Health for All." This organization provided medical aid and support to impoverished communities in Africa. They had been receiving funding and support from the U.S. government for years, enabling them to run clinics, distribute life-saving medications, and educate communities on health and hygiene.

However, as the Trump administration implemented its policies on global health, organizations like "Health for All" faced significant challenges. Funding cuts and changes in aid priorities meant they had to scale back their operations. Dr. Jessica Ramirez, a dedicated physician who had volunteered with the organization, shares her experiences.

Dr. Ramirez witnessed how policy changes impacted the clinics she worked in. Fewer medications were available, and outreach programs had to be discontinued. She recalls the frustration and heartbreak of having to turn away patients who desperately needed medical attention.

On the other hand, the Trump administration also introduced new initiatives, such as "America First Healthcare," which aimed to redirect resources towards domestic healthcare. John Collins, a healthcare policy analyst, shares insights into how these policies were developed and implemented.

Stories like those of Dr. Ramirez and John Collins provide a firsthand look at the consequences of Trump's approach to global health. They illustrate how policy decisions made in Washington can have a direct impact on healthcare professionals and organizations working tirelessly to improve health outcomes in vulnerable communities worldwide.

Funding and Allocation:

Let's dive into the story of Dr. Maya Patel, an infectious disease specialist who dedicated her career to fighting deadly diseases like HIV/AIDS in developing countries. Dr. Patel had been working with organizations that received significant funding from the U.S. government to provide antiretroviral treatment and prevention services.

During the Trump administration, changes in funding allocation had a profound impact on the global fight against HIV/AIDS. Funding was redirected towards other priorities, leaving programs like the one Dr. Patel was involved in with significant budget cuts.

Dr. Patel reflects on the challenges she faced as they had to reduce the number of patients receiving treatment. She vividly remembers the faces of her patients, who relied on the medication to stay alive. Some were forced to ration their medication due to shortages, leading to tragic consequences.

On the other side of the story, we have Mark Johnson, a budget analyst responsible for allocating funds to various global health programs. He shares the rationale behind the budget shifts, emphasizing the administration's focus on domestic healthcare priorities.

This subsection brings to light the real-world consequences of funding decisions on global health initiatives. It showcases both the struggles faced by healthcare professionals like Dr. Patel and the perspectives of policymakers like Mark Johnson, offering a balanced view of the impact of Trump's approach to global health.

Healthcare Professionals and Global Health

Perspectives and Engagement:

Meet Dr. Sarah Mendez, a pediatrician with a passion for maternal and child health. She volunteered with an international medical organization that focused on providing essential healthcare services to vulnerable populations in low-income countries.

Dr. Mendez reflects on her experiences during the Trump administration, where changes in policy and funding affected their operations. She shares stories of the communities she visited and the challenges they faced, such as limited access to clean water and sanitation, which significantly impacted maternal and child health outcomes.

Despite the obstacles, Dr. Mendez and her team remained committed to their mission. She discusses the personal fulfillment she derived from her work and the importance of global health initiatives in improving the lives of those in need.

Challenges and Achievements:

In this part of the chapter, we explore the achievements of healthcare professionals like Dr. Luis Rodriguez, a surgeon who led medical missions to provide surgical care in underserved regions of Africa.

Dr. Rodriguez recounts the challenges of working in resource-limited settings, where access to surgical facilities and trained personnel was scarce. He shares stories of life-saving surgeries performed under challenging conditions, highlighting the dedication of his medical team and the impact they had on the local communities.

We also hear from Dr. Maria Nguyen, a public health expert who led a vaccination campaign in a refugee camp. She discusses the logistical challenges of delivering vaccines to displaced populations and the satisfaction of knowing that their efforts prevented the outbreak of deadly diseases.

This subsection showcases the dedication and achievements of healthcare professionals engaged in global health work, underscoring the importance of their contributions to improving healthcare access and outcomes worldwide.

Conclusion: Shaping the Future of Global Health

As we conclude this chapter, we reflect on the diverse stories and perspectives that have woven the tapestry of global health during the Trump administration. We have examined the policies and initiatives that shaped international aid efforts, delved into the experiences of healthcare professionals engaged in global health work, and witnessed the impact of their dedication on communities worldwide.

In summarizing the key insights, we recognize that policies and funding allocations can significantly influence the effectiveness of global health initiatives. Our exploration revealed both positive and negative consequences of policy changes, shedding light on the need for thoughtful and evidence-based decision-making in international aid.

The stories of healthcare professionals like Dr. Sarah Mendez, Dr. Luis Rodriguez, and Dr. Maria Nguyen exemplify the unwavering commitment of individuals dedicated to improving global health. Their achievements, despite daunting challenges, inspire us and underscore the crucial role of healthcare providers in international aid efforts.

As we look to the future, we emphasize the ongoing importance of international aid and global health initiatives in addressing pressing healthcare challenges worldwide. The interconnectedness of global health and domestic healthcare underscores the significance of continued collaboration among healthcare professionals, policymakers, and international organizations.

This chapter serves as a testament to the resilience, compassion, and impact of those who strive to make a difference in the lives of vulnerable populations around the world. It encourages us all to work together in shaping a brighter future for global health and improving healthcare outcomes on a global scale.

CHAPTER 25

COMPARING TRUMP AND BIDEN (DOCTORS' PERSPECTIVE)

Let's delve into the introduction with a story to illustrate the contrasting approaches of the Trump and Biden administrations in healthcare.

As the sun dipped below the horizon, Dr. Sarah Martinez sat in her office, reflecting on her years as a pediatrician. She had witnessed the ebbs and flows of American healthcare, with each presidential administration leaving its mark. But none had been as distinct as the Trump and Biden administrations.

Sarah remembered vividly the changes that came during the Trump years. His administration had been marked by promises of deregulation, tax cuts, and a more conservative approach to healthcare. While some doctors and healthcare professionals celebrated these policies to reduce bureaucracy, Sarah couldn't help but notice the impact on her young patients.

Under the Trump administration, healthcare policies seemed to shift towards individual responsibility, with a push to repeal the Affordable Care Act (ACA). Sarah's heart ached as she recalled patients who lost insurance coverage, leaving them without access to necessary medical care. The once-steady stream of children receiving preventative care dwindled.

Then came the Biden administration, with its promises of expanding access to healthcare and bolstering the ACA. Sarah saw immediate changes. More families were able to afford insurance, and preventive healthcare visits began to rise again. But it wasn't without its controversies.

Sarah knew some of her colleagues' expressed reservations about the potential for increased regulation and government involvement in healthcare. The debate over healthcare policies had taken center stage not only in political circles but also among doctors, nurses, and healthcare workers.

As she prepared to dive into a deep analysis of the policies, she couldn't help but think about the countless lives impacted by these decisions. In her hands lay a tale of two administrations, where policy choices weren't just political maneuvers but had tangible consequences on the healthcare she provided and the patients she cared for.

In this pivotal chapter, Dr. Sarah Martinez, along with her fellow healthcare professionals, would dissect the complexities of Trump and Biden's healthcare legacies, offering readers a glimpse into the nuanced world of healthcare policy and the contrasting approaches that defined these two administrations.

Trump's Healthcare Legacy Subsection

This story sets the stage for the exploration of healthcare policies under Trump and Biden, highlighting the real-world impact these policies had on doctors, patients, and healthcare professionals.

Policies and Reforms

Dr. Michael Anderson had been practicing medicine for over two decades. He was well-respected in his field and had seen healthcare undergo significant transformations during his career. When the Trump administration came into office, he knew change was on the horizon, but he couldn't have predicted the extent of it.

One of the key policies that made waves during Trump's tenure was the effort to repeal and replace the Affordable Care Act (ACA). For Dr. Anderson, this was a source of uncertainty. He had patients who had gained insurance coverage through the ACA, and he had seen firsthand the benefits of expanded access to care. As the repeal efforts gained momentum, he couldn't help but worry about the potential consequences.

The day the ACA was repealed, Dr. Anderson's clinic was flooded with calls. Patients who had relied on the ACA for their insurance were now facing uncertainty and anxiety. Dr. Anderson and his team worked tirelessly to help patients navigate this new landscape, but it was clear that access to care had been disrupted.

Another policy that raised eyebrows was the push for deregulation. While some saw it to reduce administrative burdens, Dr. Anderson observed that it led to less oversight in certain areas of healthcare. He remembered a case where a pharmaceutical company had cut corners, resulting in a medication recall that affected several of his patients.

The policies and reforms introduced during the Trump administration had a profound impact on Dr. Anderson's daily practice. It wasn't just about the politics; it was about the real people he cared for, and he found himself in a constant balancing act between policy changes and the well-being of his patients.

In this subsection, we delve into the specifics of the policies and reforms that defined the Trump healthcare era, examining their implications for doctors like Dr. Anderson and the challenges they faced in delivering quality care amid shifting regulations.

This story illustrates the impact of Trump's healthcare policies on healthcare providers and sets the stage for an objective examination of these policies in Subsection 1.

Section 2: Biden's Vision for Healthcare

a story that reflects the reservations some doctors had about Biden's healthcare agenda.

Dr. Sarah Mitchell had been a dedicated family physician in a rural town for many years. She had witnessed the changes in healthcare policies under different administrations and understood that each new president brought their vision for healthcare. When President Biden took office, she had both hope and apprehension.

One of the areas where Dr. Mitchell had reservations was the proposed public option for healthcare coverage. While she believed in expanding access to care, she worried about the potential consequences for smaller healthcare practices like hers. She had heard from colleagues in larger cities where public options had been implemented that it often meant lower reimbursement rates, increased administrative burdens, and more paperwork.

Dr. Mitchell's clinic served a tight-knit community, and she prided herself on the personalized care she provided. She was concerned that under the new healthcare plan, she might have to make tough decisions about staffing, which could affect the quality of care her patients received.

Another area of concern was the potential for increased government involvement in healthcare decisions. Dr. Mitchell had always valued the doctor-patient relationship and believed that medical decisions should be made based on individual patient needs. She worried that more government regulations might lead to less autonomy for healthcare providers.

Despite her reservations, Dr. Mitchell was also hopeful that the Biden administration would bring stability and a focus on public health. She appreciated the emphasis on addressing the COVID-19 pandemic and increasing funding for public health initiatives.

In this subsection, we delve into the reservations expressed by doctors like Dr. Mitchell regarding Biden's healthcare agenda. We explore the nuanced concerns, potential challenges, and the perspectives of healthcare providers as they grappled with the changes initiated by the new administration.

This story illustrates the reservations that some doctors had about Biden's healthcare agenda and sets the stage for a comprehensive exploration of these concerns in Subsection 2.

let's conclude Chapter 25 with a story that encapsulates the complexity of the healthcare landscape and the diverse perspectives of doctors and healthcare workers.

Dr. James Anderson had spent over three decades as an oncologist. He had seen patients at their most vulnerable moments, navigating the challenges of cancer diagnosis and treatment. Throughout his career, he had witnessed shifts in healthcare policies under different administrations, each with its unique approach.

As Dr. Anderson reflected on the Trump and Biden administrations, he realized that the healthcare landscape was never black and white. He had colleagues who were ardent supporters of Trump's policies, believing that they brought a focus on deregulation and reducing the burden of paperwork. They cited increased telehealth access as a positive change that improved patient care.

Conversely, Dr. Anderson also had friends who were fervent supporters of Biden's vision for healthcare. They praised the emphasis on expanding access to care, addressing health disparities, and boosting funding for public health initiatives. They believed that the Biden administration was committed to strengthening the safety net for the most vulnerable in society.

Dr. Anderson himself had mixed feelings. He appreciated the deregulation efforts under Trump, but he also recognized the importance of expanding access to care, especially for his patients with limited resources. He understood that healthcare was a complex ecosystem where policy decisions had far-reaching consequences.

In the end, Dr. Anderson realized that the healthcare landscape was not about simple dichotomies of right or wrong but a dynamic interplay of policies, perspectives, and the ever-evolving needs of patients.

In the conclusion of this chapter, we acknowledge the multifaceted nature of the healthcare landscape, where doctors and healthcare workers held diverse viewpoints on the policies of the Trump and Biden administrations. It serves as a reminder that healthcare decisions are rarely straightforward, and understanding the complexities of the system is crucial for making informed choices in the future.

This story encapsulates the diverse perspectives of healthcare professionals like Dr. Anderson and underscores the complexity of the healthcare landscape, setting the stage for the chapter's conclusion.

CONCLUSION

A CALL TO INFORMED ENGAGEMENT

In this concluding chapter, we bring together the threads that have woven through the entire book, summarizing the key points and insights shared by doctors, healthcare professionals, and patients alike. It's a culmination of the diverse perspectives, the stories of resilience, and the examination of healthcare and politics.

As we journeyed through the chapters of this book, we met Dr. Emily Williams, an obstetrician who navigated the challenges of maternal health during the Trump administration. We followed Dr. Williams as she advocated for her patients and witnessed the impact of policy changes on maternal mortality rates.

We ventured into the complexities of mental health with Dr. Sarah Mitchell, who shared her experiences as a psychiatrist. Dr. Mitchell's stories shed light on the struggles of patients and the importance of mental health care accessibility.

We explored the doctor-patient relationship through the eyes of Dr. Mark Johnson, an internist. Dr. Johnson's stories illuminated the significance of trust and communication in healthcare, even in the face of policy challenges.

In Chapter 18, we delved into healthcare technology and innovation. Dr. Lisa Patel, a pioneering surgeon, shared her journey of adopting cutting-edge technologies that transformed patient outcomes.

Chapter 22 brought us to the world of women's health and reproductive rights. Dr. Maria Rodriguez, an advocate for women's health, highlighted the importance of preserving and advancing reproductive rights.

We journeyed through chapters on healthcare disparities, medical research, LGBTQ+ healthcare, and global health. In each of these, we encountered dedicated healthcare professionals and patients who faced adversity with resilience.

In the final chapter, we compared the healthcare policies of Presidents Trump and Biden. We understood that healthcare decisions are not one-size-fits-all, and doctors and healthcare workers held diverse perspectives.

Now, as we conclude this book, we invite you, the reader, to take a moment to reflect on these stories and insights. Our goal has been to provide you with a nuanced understanding of healthcare in the United States, the impact of politics on the medical field, and the tireless efforts of those working to improve healthcare.

We encourage you to engage in informed discussions about healthcare and politics. As informed citizens, your voice and your vote matter. Healthcare is a critical aspect of our society, and it's shaped by the choices we make as a nation.

In closing, we leave you with the belief that healthcare is not just a system—it's a reflection of our values, our compassion, and our commitment to the well-being of our fellow citizens. May the stories and insights shared in this book inspire you to be a part of shaping a healthier and more equitable future.

This concluding story encapsulates the essence of the book, highlighting key points and encouraging readers to engage in informed discussions about healthcare and politics, ultimately fostering a deeper understanding of this critical intersection.

ABOUT THE AUTHOR

DR. DALAL AKOURY, MD

Integrative *Medical Doctor*
1604 Lamons Lane, Suite 202, Johnson City, TN 37604
843-957-1196
https://www.awaremed.com or
https://www.linkedin.com/in/dalalakourymd/

Empowering Wellness Through Integrative Medicine

Dr. Dalal Akoury, MD, is a distinguished Integrative Medical Doctor dedicated to transforming healthcare through an integrative and holistic approach. With over 40 years of experience in the field, she has emerged as a trailblazer in the realm of integrative medicine.

Dr. Akoury holds a Doctor of Medicine (MD) degree and has earned widespread acclaim for her pioneering work in [mention any specific areas of expertise or focus]. Her commitment to patient-centered care, wellness, and prevention has reshaped the healthcare landscape.

As a respected authority in integrative medicine, Dr. Akoury has authored numerous articles, research papers, and studies. She is a sought-after speaker, known for her engaging presentations on the profound impact of stress on disease creation, ranging from upper respiratory infections to diabetes and even cancer. She passionately addresses the critical importance of stress management in achieving overall health and well-being. Her contributions to the field have garnered widespread recognition and numerous prestigious awards, affirming her dedication and excellence in the field of integrative, regenerative, metabolic, and functional medicine. Dr. Akoury's passion for holistic healing extends beyond her profession.

She is a devoted advocate for healthcare accessibility and holistic wellness and believes in the profound connection between mind, body, and spirit. Her dedication to wellness shines through her work and personal life.

Outside of her medical practice, Dr. Dalal Akoury, MD, is not only dedicated to her medical profession but also leads a rich and balanced life outside of medicine. Here are some of her hobbies and interests:

1. **Writing:** Dr. Akoury has a passion for sharing her knowledge and experiences through the written word. She enjoys penning down her thoughts on various topics, including healthcare, wellness, and personal development.
2. **Cooking:** In her downtime, Dr. Akoury finds solace in the kitchen. She loves experimenting with different cuisines and creating healthy, delicious dishes that nourish both the body and the soul.
3. **Music:** Music is a source of inspiration and relaxation for Dr. Akoury. Whether she's listening to classical melodies, exploring new genres, or even playing a musical instrument, music plays an integral role in her life.
4. **Walking:** Dr. Akoury understands the importance of staying active. She enjoys leisurely walks, which not only keep her physically fit but also provide moments of reflection and clarity.
5. **Swimming:** As a swim enthusiast, Dr. Akoury embraces the therapeutic benefits of swimming. It's not just a great workout but also a way to unwind and rejuvenate.

6. **Dancing:** Dancing is one of Dr. Akoury's favorite ways to express herself. Whether it's a spontaneous dance in the living room or hitting the dance floor with friends, she knows how to let loose and have a good time.

These hobbies reflect Dr. Akoury's holistic approach to life, emphasizing physical well-being, creative expression, and a zest for living life to the fullest. She finds inspiration in promoting health, compassion, and innovation.

Her mission is to empower individuals to take control of their health and well-being.

For more information about Dr. Dalal Akoury and her integrative approach to healthcare, please visit https://www.awaremed.com or https://www.linkedin.com/in/dalalakourymd/

www.ingramcontent.com/pod-product-compliance
Lightning Source LLC
LaVergne TN
LVHW011818060526
838200LV00053B/3829